Diversify
& Prosper

Jean Kristensen

Diversify & Prosper

BUILDING A SUCCESSFUL
SUPPLIER DIVERSITY
PROGRAM

Advantage | Books

Published by Advantage Books, Charleston, South Carolina.
An imprint of Advantage Media.

ADVANTAGE is a registered trademark, and the Advantage colophon is a trademark of Advantage Media Group, Inc.

Printed in the United States of America.

10 9 8 7 6 5 4 3 2 1

ISBN: 978-1-64225-592-8 (Paperback)
ISBN: 978-1-64225-591-1 (eBook)

Library of Congress Control Number: 2024904610

Cover design by Megan Elger.
Layout design by Matthew Morse.

This publication is designed to provide accurate and authoritative information in regard to the subject matter covered. It is sold with the understanding that the publisher is not engaged in rendering legal, accounting, or other professional services. If legal advice or other expert assistance is required, the services of a competent professional person should be sought.

Advantage Books is an imprint of Advantage Media Group. Advantage Media helps busy entrepreneurs, CEOs, and leaders write and publish a book to grow their business and become the authority in their field. Advantage authors comprise an exclusive community of industry professionals, idea-makers, and thought leaders. For more information go to **advantagemedia.com**.

I want to dedicate this book to my brother, Gregory JWK Stimphil (1/10/74 – 5/7/2024) whose life was cut short too soon. Gregory was an amazing human full of love, courage, and ambition. As a Black male who was disabled, he faced enormous challenges. Through this book, I hope to raise awareness, inspire our corporate partners/government to understand the impact that supplier diversity can have on a person like Greg and others who face similar challenges.

Contents

Introduction

In a world of boundless opportunities and a myriad of voices, supplier diversity emerges as a powerful catalyst for change—a realm where businesses, communities, and aspirations intertwine in a tapestry of transformation. As the founder and CEO of JKA Solutions, my journey into the realm of supplier diversity has been a relentless pursuit of equity, inclusion, and empowerment. This book is a heartfelt invitation to join me on this transformative odyssey—one that reveals the intricate layers of supplier diversity and emboldens readers to navigate its complexities with confidence.

From the earliest chapters of my life story, I witnessed the relentless pursuit of the American dream through my parents—a Haitian father and a Danish mother—united by love and a shared determination to thrive in an unfamiliar land. Their resilience in the face of adversity, coupled with my father's ventures as an entrepreneur, laid the foundation for my unwavering commitment to making a difference. Today, I am propelled by a burning passion to elevate supplier diversity from a mere checkbox to an empowering force that drives economic impact and cultivates a sense of belonging for diverse businesses.

Supplier diversity is more than just a business strategy; it is an instrument of change that resonates with the very essence of my being. Through JKA Solutions, we have been devoted to mentoring, empowering, and uplifting local and diverse suppliers, fostering a thriving ecosystem of equitable opportunities. Our unwavering dedication to supplier diversity is not only a testament to our values but also an embodiment of the change we wish to see in the world.

This book is an intimate portrayal of my experiences—the triumphs, the challenges, and the lessons that have shaped my perspective on supplier diversity. My mission is to inspire and empower you, the reader, by sharing practical insights and strategies that transcend the complexities of supplier diversity. I believe that through knowledge and understanding, we can collectively harness the true power of supplier diversity to create sustainable, long-lasting impacts.

In the dynamic landscape of supplier diversity, mixed feelings often cloud the vision of progress. As you embark on this journey, I aim to unveil the true essence of supplier diversity, unraveling its intricacies with transparency and authenticity. Together, we will confront the obstacles head-on, embracing the beauty of diversity and fostering an environment where diverse businesses flourish.

To those who seek to create a lasting impact within their organizations and communities, I extend my hand and heart as a guide in this empowering expedition. Supplier diversity is not merely a means to an end; it is an ongoing journey of transformation—a symphony of opportunity, equity, and growth.

As we probe into the chapters ahead, I invite you to embrace this voyage with an open mind and a courageous heart. Let us celebrate the multifaceted beauty of supplier diversity and seize the transformative power it holds. Together, we will empower, uplift, and inspire, leaving a profound legacy of inclusivity and prosperity for generations to come. This book is not just my story. It is our collective journey as we unravel the true potential of supplier diversity.

In the pages that follow, we will traverse uncharted territories, driven by the conviction that supplier diversity is not merely complex; it is a boundless wellspring of opportunity waiting to be explored. As we journey together, let us forge ahead with determination, compassion, and an unwavering belief in the immense possibilities that lie ahead.

Welcome to the transformative world of supplier diversity—where empowerment becomes a guiding star, illuminating the path to inclusive success.

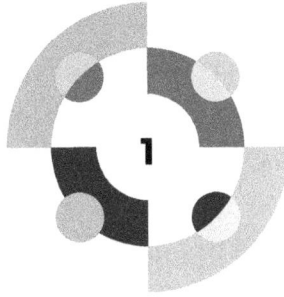

Understanding Supplier Diversity

A community is a beautiful blend of unique individuals, each contributing their own perspectives, experiences, and backgrounds. It's about recognizing and appreciating the diversity in race, gender identities, sexual preferences, socioeconomic status, positions of service, physical abilities, incarceration status, and more. To create a thriving community, we need representation and inclusivity in our local government and organizations. When we embrace the differences among us, we can build a stronger and more united community where everyone feels valued and included. Supplier diversity programs are a tool that helps bring support to this mission.

Whenever I am approached by a potential new client, I remind them that supplier diversity programs are nothing new; they've been around for nearly four decades. In 1953, The Small Business Act established the United States Small Business Administration (SBA) to help develop businesses and provide assistance to minorities and other disadvantaged groups. But it would take a while for things to gather some steam.

When I think about the history of supplier diversity, I'm reminded of the trailblazers who laid the foundation for this important movement. Companies like IBM and Xerox were among the early adopters of supplier diversity programs, recognizing the significance of promoting economic opportunities for minority-owned businesses.

IBM and Xerox set the stage for supplier diversity in the late 1960s and early 1970s. During this period, affirmative action played a pivotal role in addressing historical disadvantages faced by minority communities. In response to the civil rights movement and the need for increased diversity and inclusion, these corporations took action to create opportunities for minority-owned businesses.

The National Minority Supplier Development Council (NMSDC) and the Women's Business Enterprise National Council (WBENC) emerged as key players in formalizing supplier diversity efforts. In 1972, the NMSDC was established to foster economic growth for minority entrepreneurs. They introduced a certification process to verify the minority status of businesses seeking access to corporate procurement opportunities.

Similarly, in 1997, the WBENC was founded to advocate for women-owned businesses and their inclusion in corporate supply chains. Their certification program became the hallmark of recognition for women-owned businesses seeking to engage with major corporations.

Both NMSDC and WBENC certifications involve rigorous assessments to ensure that businesses meet the required ownership, management, and control criteria. These certifications not only provide a formal stamp of recognition but also open doors to a network of corporate partners. Diverse suppliers gain access to new business connections and opportunities through these affiliations.

In the 1980s, the traction of supplier diversity gained momentum as corporations increasingly recognized the benefits of a diverse supplier base. Legislative support for supplier diversity came through the Federal Acquisition Streamlining Act (FASA), enacted in 1994. The FASA required federal agencies to establish goals for small business procurement and subcontracting opportunities, giving diverse suppliers greater visibility in government contracting.

While acknowledging the significant progress made by companies like IBM and Xerox and the establishment of certification programs by NMSDC and WBENC, it is essential to recognize that the approach to supplier diversity has not seen significant changes in recent times. As we explore this topic further in the book, we'll explore deeper into the current state of supplier diversity and the need for innovative approaches to drive even greater economic inclusion. However, as we continue on our journey to strengthen supplier diversity, we must also acknowledge that there is still much work to be done. The landscape of supplier diversity has evolved, but it is crucial to assess the effectiveness of current strategies and explore new avenues for progress.

This book will examine the challenges faced by diverse suppliers and the obstacles that persist in accessing corporate procurement opportunities. By examining the current landscape and learning from the successes and setbacks of the past, we can develop strategies to drive meaningful change and create a more equitable and prosperous future for all.

Through comprehensive research and insights from industry experts, we aim to shed light on innovative approaches that can disrupt the status quo and foster greater economic inclusion. Supplier diversity should not be seen as a mere checkbox or a token gesture; instead, it should be an integral part of an organization's core values and long-term growth strategy.

As we move forward, let us draw inspiration from the pioneers who paved the way and use their legacy as a catalyst for transformative change. By collaborating and reimagining the supplier diversity landscape, we can build a more inclusive business ecosystem that benefits not only diverse suppliers but also the organizations they partner with and the communities they serve.

Despite the progress made, it is still exceedingly challenging for small, diverse suppliers to access the corporate supply chain. This presents a perplexing situation, as one would anticipate that greater strides would have been achieved by now. To establish sustainable supplier diversity programs, we must redirect the conversation toward emphasizing diversity, supporting small businesses, and empowering local communities. It is disheartening to witness the lack of significant advancements in this area since the 1970s, especially when considering the remarkable progress witnessed in numerous other industries. Supplier diversity continues to pose significant obstacles for many organizations, necessitating a proactive exploration of strategies to overcome these barriers and foster genuine inclusivity.

In my opinion, one of the main reasons why supplier diversity remains a significant challenge for many organizations is the inherent complexities of doing business with large corporations. There seems to be a notable disconnect between these organizations and small, diverse suppliers in terms of understanding how to effectively collaborate. The intricacies of navigating corporate procurement processes, meeting specific requirements, and establishing mutually beneficial relationships can be overwhelming for small suppliers. This lack of knowledge and experience in engaging with larger entities often acts as a barrier, preventing diverse suppliers from accessing the corporate supply chain.

Furthermore, discrimination also plays a role in exacerbating these challenges. Despite the progress made in promoting diversity and inclusion, biases and preconceived notions still persist within corporate structures. Diverse suppliers may face unfair scrutiny, skepticism, or limited opportunities simply because of their minority status. This discrimination can hinder their ability to compete on an equal footing and secure contracts, despite possessing the necessary qualifications and capabilities. Overcoming these discriminatory barriers is crucial to fostering a truly inclusive and equitable supplier diversity landscape.

When we look at the history of supplier diversity programs, it's clear that they face certain challenges. However, there are avenues we can explore to make these programs more effective. One idea that resonates with me is for corporations to actively consider local businesses as part of their supplier diversity efforts. By embracing local businesses, corporations can tap into their unique expertise and offerings while simultaneously empowering the communities they operate in. This approach not only diversifies the supplier base but also fuels local economies and fosters a sense of shared success. Including local businesses as a viable option within supplier diversity programs can open doors for diverse suppliers and create a positive ripple effect. It's an opportunity for corporations to make a real impact while championing diversity and community growth.

Supplier Diversity Beyond Race and Gender

Supplier diversity programs have made significant strides in promoting economic inclusion and creating opportunities for diverse businesses beyond the traditional focus on race and gender. In recent years, there has been increasing recognition of the importance of supporting LGBTQ and veteran-owned businesses, leading to the emergence of programs specifically tailored to their needs.

The push for supplier diversity programs to include LGBTQ and veteran-owned businesses stems from the understanding that diversity encompasses a broad spectrum of identities and experiences. Recognizing the unique challenges faced by these groups in the business world, organizations and governments alike have taken steps to level the playing field and provide them with greater access to procurement opportunities.

The journey toward LGBTQ supplier diversity programs began in the 1980s, when IBM and Xerox took the lead in establishing supplier diversity initiatives. However, it wasn't until the late 1990s and early 2000s that the conversation expanded to include LGBTQ-owned businesses. The National Gay and Lesbian Chamber of Commerce (NGLCC) played a crucial role in driving this progress, advocating for the economic empowerment of LGBTQ entrepreneurs.

In 2002, the NGLCC introduced its Supplier Diversity Initiative, aiming to increase opportunities for LGBTQ-owned businesses to participate in corporate procurement. The NGLCC developed a certification process to verify the LGBTQ ownership status of businesses, providing them with a valuable credential recognized by major corporations seeking diverse suppliers.

As the awareness of LGBTQ supplier diversity grew, many corporations realized the value of incorporating LGBTQ-owned businesses into their supply chains. These businesses not only bring unique perspectives and innovative ideas but also foster an inclusive environment that aligns with the values of many customers and stakeholders.

Similarly, the recognition of the sacrifices and contributions made by veterans led to the establishment of supplier diversity programs for veteran-owned businesses. In the early 2000s, organizations like the National Veteran-Owned Business Association (NaVOBA) emerged to advocate for the economic advancement of veteran entrepreneurs.

The NaVOBA introduced the Buy Veteran program, which aimed to connect corporations with veteran-owned businesses. The program involved certifying veteran-owned businesses and providing corporations with a vetted pool of suppliers that share a commitment to service and excellence. Furthermore, the government played a pivotal role in supporting veteran-owned businesses through the Veterans Benefits Act of 2003. The legislation required federal agencies to set aside a percentage of contracts for service-disabled, veteran-owned small businesses (SDVOSBs), further advancing their access to procurement opportunities.

These programs have not only created economic opportunities for LGBTQ and veteran-owned businesses but also fostered a sense of pride and recognition within these communities. Supplier diversity initiatives have empowered LGBTQ and veteran entrepreneurs to grow their businesses, hire more employees, and contribute to the economic well-being of their communities.

Supplier diversity programs have made significant progress in promoting diversity and inclusion by expanding their focus beyond traditional categories of race, gender, and ethnicity. One area that has gained increasing attention is supplier diversity programs that aim to support businesses owned by people with disabilities. These programs play a crucial role in creating economic opportunities and empowering individuals with disabilities to thrive in the business world.

The journey toward supplier diversity for people with disabilities began with the recognition that this segment of the population faces unique challenges in accessing business opportunities. Despite the significant contributions they can make, they have historically encountered barriers to entrepreneurship, such as lack of access to capital, training, and networking opportunities.

In response to these challenges, organizations and governments have taken steps to foster a more inclusive business environment. Supplier diversity programs for people with disabilities aim to level the playing field and provide them with access to procurement opportunities that were previously out of reach.

One of the organizations at the forefront of this movement is Disability:IN (formerly known as the US Business Leadership Network), a nonprofit organization that advocates for the inclusion of people with disabilities in the workplace, supply chain, and marketplace. Disability:IN has developed a certification process that verifies businesses as Disability-Owned Business Enterprises (DOBEs). This certification provides businesses owned by individuals with disabilities with a valuable credential that opens doors to corporate procurement opportunities.

In addition to certification programs, they provide resources and support to DOBEs, helping them navigate the complexities of supplier diversity and build mutually beneficial relationships with corporations seeking diverse suppliers. Through educational programs, networking events, and mentorship opportunities, DOBEs gain the knowledge and skills necessary to thrive in a competitive marketplace.

In the realm of supplier diversity programs, it is essential to recognize the notable strides made beyond the conventional focus on race and gender. Several initiatives play a significant role in fostering economic inclusion for diverse groups. Let us delve into three of these critical programs: Disadvantaged Business Enterprises (DBE), Historically Underutilized Business Zone (HubZone), and Small Disadvantaged Businesses (SDB).

The DBE program holds particular significance, especially within the transportation sector. This initiative seeks to provide socially and economically disadvantaged businesses with equitable opportunities to secure contracts and participate in transportation infrastructure projects. The DBE certification serves as a catalyst for entrepreneurs facing economic barriers, allowing them to contribute meaningfully to crucial infrastructure development.

The HubZone program, administered by the US SBA, is noteworthy for its focus on stimulating economic growth in historically underutilized regions. This program's dedication to empowering communities and fostering development is commendable. By encouraging businesses to invest in distressed areas, the HubZone program not only generates employment opportunities but also revitalizes these regions with newfound prospects.

The SDB program, a part of the 8(a) Business Development program, stands out for its consideration of the social and economic disadvantages faced by business owners, irrespective of their race or gender. SDB certification empowers these businesses to overcome barriers and succeed in the competitive marketplace. Beyond providing a competitive edge in securing federal contracts, the program offers invaluable mentorship and training, nurturing growth and development.

In the realm of supplier diversity efforts, some organizations have embraced a unique approach that prioritizes the use of local businesses, making a significant impact on the communities they serve. This practice involves a deliberate focus on engaging and supporting businesses within specific geographic areas, often determined by zip codes, without requiring formal certifications. Notably, anchor institutions like Columbia University have embraced this strategy, recognizing the manifold of benefits it offers to both the local economy and the institution itself.

Columbia, located in the heart of New York City, is one such organization that has effectively implemented this approach to supplier diversity. As an anchor institution, the university recognizes its profound influence on the surrounding community and seeks to leverage its procurement power to foster economic growth and social equity in the neighborhoods it serves.

By prioritizing local businesses through zip code-based preferences, Columbia strategically bolsters economic development in nearby communities. This localized focus enables the institution to establish deeper connections with businesses in its immediate vicinity, cultivating a sense of partnership and shared prosperity. They recognize that supporting local enterprises creates a ripple effect, leading to job creation, enhanced business capacities, and improved livelihoods for residents.

One of the key advantages to this approach is its flexibility and accessibility. Local businesses, particularly smaller enterprises, may face challenges in obtaining formal certifications or meeting stringent eligibility criteria imposed by some supplier diversity programs. By adopting a zip code-based path, organizations can embrace a more inclusive strategy that extends support to a broader range of businesses, including those in underserved or marginalized communities.

While the zip code-based model does not involve formal certification processes, organizations like Columbia do maintain rigorous supplier evaluation procedures to ensure the quality and reliability of their local partners.

When we think about local businesses, we envision more than just the familiar coffee shop on the corner or the quaint family-owned restaurant down the street. They encompass a wide range of enterprises, including administrative services, project management firms, printing companies, art studios, and food and beverage establishments. These companies play a crucial role in our local economies, contributing to the unique character and vitality of our communities.

What's truly remarkable about these local businesses is that they often reflect the diverse tapestry of our society. They are founded and run by individuals from various backgrounds and communities. Consider the statistics: as of October 2021, around 18.7 percent of all businesses, totaling 1.1 million enterprises, are owned by minorities. Veterans proudly own 5.7 percent, representing approximately 331,151 businesses, while women-owned businesses make up an impressive 20.9 percent, encompassing 1.2 million establishments.[1] It's important to recognize that there may be some overlap among these demographics.

Now imagine the potential when we bring these local businesses into the corporate supply chain. By actively seeking partnerships and collaborations with them, corporations can tap into a rich pool of diverse suppliers. Not only does this promote economic empowerment for local entrepreneurs, but it also injects fresh perspectives, creativity, and innovation into the supply chain. The ripple effects of

---

[1]   "Data on minority-owned, veteran-owned and women-owned businesses," census. gov, March 14, 2022, https://www.census.gov/newsroom/press-releases/2021/ annual-business-survey.html.

such collaborations extend beyond business transactions; they nurture a sense of community, foster economic resilience, and create a more inclusive and equitable business ecosystem.

In the course of building your program, you may get asked how inclusive procurement can spur job growth. The Greater New Haven Chamber of Commerce in Connecticut is now partnering with individuals who were previously incarcerated and using them as a potential labor pool. As it turns out, folks who were formally incarcerated experience an unemployment rate over 27 percent.[2] Nobody wants to hire them—but now, we are seeing corporations shift their thinking around those types of individuals.

The same is true for folks with disabilities. Among the disabled, a large portion of people consider their primary issue to be their mobility. That obviously does not mean they cannot do other things. So when we talk about sparing job growth, there are clearly opportunities.

That is one of the benefits to having a diverse and inclusive supplier chain: It creates jobs.

When I started my company, I was the only one involved—a solo entrepreneur. I had an opportunity early on where I performed well, and that led to a scenario where I could hire more people, so that is exactly what I did. And when I hired, I hired a diverse group. Providing access and resources to small, diverse companies allows those companies to in turn provide access and resources to other minorities, be it through new contracts, additional jobs, or even just visibility in the community. The circle continues, as it were.

Just take a moment and go to the mall, a grocery store, or anywhere else you typically find large groups of people. We are no

---

2   Sarah K.S. Shannon, Christopher Uggen, Jason Schnittker, Melissa Thompson, Sara Wakefield, and Michael Massoglia "The growth, scope, and spatial distribution of people with felony records in the United States, 1948–2010," shannons.us, http://sarah.shannons.us/uploads/4/9/3/4/4934545/shannon_etal_2017_demography.pdf.

longer a country that is easily delineated by a couple of colors. By the time 2050 rolls around, the population of the United States is going to be primarily a group made up of diverse individuals.[3] Basically, white people will no longer be the majority.

Think about how that is going to impact the job market. Corporations need to get ahead of this now and become more inclusive. If not, the threat to corporate America is getting left behind and having no workers to work for them. But the companies that do get onboard with diversity and inclusion are going to need systems in place for customers, employees, and, yes, vendors to engage with.

But really, having diverse and local suppliers just makes sense. According to the SBA, 64 percent of all new jobs created in the United States are done by small businesses.[4] And if those small businesses look like the world of today and tomorrow—diverse—then your suppliers will also be diverse. And that is also the danger of the whole situation. If we are not thinking about how we can support these small businesses, we are going to create a larger, greater divide. That is unsustainable.

This is not going to disappear; it is a trend that is gaining momentum. For a corporation to be able to sustain itself, it needs to pay attention to that. Job growth is going to change dramatically as the population changes. Corporate America needs to consider it as well, because, after all, everything boils down to their customers. If they have money to spend, they will want to spend it with companies that reflect their values. Corporations that do not will fall behind.

---

3   Jonathan Vespa, Lauren Medina, and David M. Armstrong, "Demographic turning points for the United States: Population projections for 2020 to 2060," US Census Bureau, issued March 2018 and revised February 2020, https://www.census.gov/content/dam/Census/library/publications/2020/demo/p25-1144.pdf.

4   SBA's Office of Advocacy, "Small business facts: Small business job creation," April 26, 2022, https://advocacy.sba.gov/2022/04/26/small-business-facts-small-business-job-creation/.

At the heart of supplier diversity lies a fundamental truth that transcends certifications and classifications: we are all simply people. Beyond the labels and designations, the individuals who run these diverse businesses are members of the same community in which your corporation or company resides. In recognizing this shared humanity, a powerful opportunity for meaningful connections emerges.

The people and businesses within your community constitute the fabric that binds the neighborhoods and streets you call home. Engaging with them as more than just suppliers opens the door to authentic partnerships that benefit both parties. As neighbors, forming connections goes beyond a transactional relationship—it becomes an investment in the growth and prosperity of the entire community.

When you take the time to truly know and understand the diverse businesses in your locality, you gain insights into their unique challenges, aspirations, and strengths. You discover the vast potential they hold as contributors to the growth and vibrancy of the community. Supporting these businesses is not just about checking a box on a supplier diversity checklist; it is about recognizing the untapped potential and talent within your very own neighborhood.

By building bridges of connection, you create a positive feedback loop of mutual support and growth. Local businesses thrive when they secure contracts and partnerships within their own community, leading to more job opportunities and increased economic activity. This, in turn, strengthens the overall economic resilience and social fabric of the neighborhood.

Certification Programs

Certification programs and entities play a role in supplier diversity initiatives, providing official recognition to businesses owned and operated by minority and women entrepreneurs. However, it's essential to understand the specific requirements and criteria set forth by each certifying organization, as they may vary based on industry, location, and ownership structure. Here is a general overview of the key requirements for getting certified as a diverse business entity:

1. *Ownership*: To be eligible for certification, a business must be at least 51 percent owned, controlled, and operated by individuals who belong to the designated diverse group. Ownership can be proven through documentation such as ownership records and tax returns.

2. *Control*: The business owner must have full operational control and decision-making authority over the company's day-to-day operations and long-term strategies.

3. *Size Criteria*: Be aware that this can vary depending on the certifying organization. Some may look at your annual revenue or the number of employees your business has.

4. *Citizenship or Legal Residency*: The certifying organization will typically require that the business owners are either US citizens or legal residents.

5. *Proof of Identity*: The owner must provide proof of identity, such as driver's licenses or passports, to verify ownership and control.

6. *Legal Business Structure*: The business structure such as a corporation, LLC, or partnership.

7. *Business Operations*: The business must be currently operational and providing goods or services.

8. *Non-Discrimination Policy*: Some certifying organizations may require that your business has a policy against discrimination based on race, gender, or other protected characteristics.

9. *Financial Records*: Businesses must provide financial statements, tax returns, or other financial records to demonstrate the business's financial viability.

These systems give you ways to find certified diverse suppliers. These are the organizations that are verified to be owned by someone who fits into the diverse definition, instead of a person who pretends to. It also adds authenticity to your supply chain, giving you more credibility among your staff and future diverse suppliers.

Let us think about the diverse supplier in the same way that we think about our employees and our customers. Who are these people? Why should they work with your organization? What is in it for them? How do you find them?

When I work with clients helping them to establish a framework for their supplier diversity programs, one of the ways we explore the definition of a diverse supplier is by examining the demographics of small businesses within the encasement area of the organization. This is a really important step, and often overlooked. The SBA, the Department of Labor, and the Census Bureau are excellent resources for helping you to understand what types of businesses are in your area. You can also work with your local municipalities and chambers of commerce, who have information on business formations, renewals, and license holders. They also can help you find those companies who have gone through diversity certification programs.

I also recommend looking at the demographics of the areas in which you are looking to expand. One of my favorite sites to use is Usafacts.com, which provides information for the changing population in terms of age, race, and population. For example, in 2020, Connecticut was more diverse than it was in 2010, and between 2010 and 2020 the share of the population that grew the most was Hispanic and

Latino, while the white (non-Hispanic) population had the largest decrease, dropping 6.1 percentage points.

As an organization, seeking to maintain market share about the changing population is a key tool that can inform your Supplier Diversity program. As you gain a deeper understanding of who lives in the community and what types of businesses are in said community, you have the framework for establishing a successful supplier diversity program. We like working with a data scientist that can append and pull data from various sources that will enable us to examine the information. I recommend exploring the data from several perspectives including race, gender, and age. I also think it is important to understand the types of businesses in the area focusing on the size and capacity. A small business can vary depending on your industry. According to the US SBA, the average revenue of a business with no employees is $44,000 per year, and the average revenue of a small business with employees is $4.9 million.[5] That results in a wide variance between the two, so do your research and see which kinds of businesses are in your area.

---

5   SBA's Office of Advocacy, "2022 Small business profiles for the states, territories, and nation," August 31, 2022, https://advocacy.sba. gov/2022/08/31/2022-small-business-profiles-for-the-states-territories-and-nation/.

2

The Business Case for Supplier Diversity

Supplier diversity is far from a charity case; it is a robust business strategy adopted by corporations to attract and retain top talent, cater to the evolving demographics of their customer base, and ignite innovation. Embracing diverse suppliers allows companies to tap into emerging markets, leading to increased market share and enhanced customer loyalty. The infusion of fresh perspectives from diverse suppliers fosters creativity and innovation within the organization, propelling it ahead in a competitive landscape.

Additionally, supplier diversity presents an opportunity for corporations to achieve cost savings through increased competition. By expanding the pool of potential vendors, businesses can enjoy more options and negotiate better deals, ultimately strengthening their supply chain. In this chapter, we will examine real-world case studies and backed statistics, offering tangible evidence of the positive impact of supplier diversity. Armed with these insights, you'll be equipped to craft a sustainable plan that drives economic growth, promotes diversity, and positions your company as a forward-thinking industry leader.

Attracting and Retaining Top Talent

As a consultant in the world of supplier diversity, I can't stress enough how important it is for companies to use it as a tool to attract and retain top talent. Let's face it, the business landscape has changed, and the new generation of professionals, the millennials and Gen Zers, care about more than just their paycheck. They want to work for companies that align with their values, especially when it comes to diversity and social responsibility.

Think about it, when you're looking for a job, don't you consider a company's commitment to diversity efforts? Well, you're not alone! Surveys show that a majority of young professionals do the same. They want to work for employers who embrace diversity and inclusion, and supplier diversity is a tangible way for companies to showcase that.

It's not just about ticking a box or meeting a quota. Supplier diversity can have a profound impact on the workforce and the company's reputation. When a company shows its dedication to working with diverse suppliers, it sends a clear message that they care about supporting minority and minority women business enterprise (MWBE). And you know what? That kind of commitment resonates with prospective employees and fosters a sense of pride and loyalty among current staff.

You see, supplier diversity goes beyond just doing the right thing; it's about creating an inclusive workplace culture where everyone feels valued and empowered. And when employees feel that way, they're more engaged, more productive, and more likely to stick around for the long haul.

But here's the thing, it's not just about the internal impact. Supplier diversity also plays a big role in how your company is perceived by the outside world. Customers are paying attention to what companies are doing in terms of diversity and social responsibility. When they see a corporation with a strong supplier diversity program, it reflects positively on the brand and can even help win new business.

It's not just about the numbers, either. Sure, diverse companies tend to perform better, but it's more than that. Supplier diversity brings in unique perspectives and skills from diverse suppliers that can spark innovation and creative problem-solving. It's about tapping into a diverse talent pool and gaining access to fresh ideas that can drive your company forward.

According to a comprehensive report by McKinsey & Company,[6] a significant 64 percent of millennials express their reluctance to work for companies that lack strong corporate social responsibility practices. Furthermore, investors are placing increasing emphasis on companies that demonstrate a robust diversity, equity, and inclusion (DEI) strategy. Remarkably, from 2016 to 2018, over $30 trillion in assets under management were allocated to firms prioritizing DEI initiatives. These statistics underscore the undeniable influence of supplier diversity on shaping a company's reputation as a desirable employer and investment destination.

The profound impact of supplier diversity extends beyond mere optics; it embodies a profound commitment to diversity and a

---

6   Milan Prilepok, Shelley Stewart III, Ken Yearwood, Ammanuel Zegeye, "Expand
     diversity among your suppliers—and add value to your organization," McKinsey &
     Company, May 17, 2022, www.mckinsey.com/capabilities/operations/our-insights/
     expand-diversity-among-your-suppliers-and-add-value-to-your-organization.

dedication to making a positive social impact. This alignment with values resonates deeply with top talent, particularly millennials, who actively seek workplaces that align with their principles. Simultaneously, supplier diversity proves to be an influential factor in attracting investors who prioritize supporting socially responsible businesses. The alignment of supplier diversity with corporate values not only drives talent attraction but also creates an attractive investment proposition.

As a seasoned supplier diversity consultant, my experience has revealed the tangible benefits that companies reap from embracing supplier diversity as a core business strategy. By championing supplier diversity, companies gain a competitive edge in the talent market and the financial world. The evidence is clear: a strategic focus on supplier diversity can elevate a corporation's standing, making it an employer of choice and an appealing investment option. Therefore, if fostering a dynamic workforce and cultivating an impressive investment profile are your strategic priorities, supplier diversity warrants a prominent place in your business agenda.

Changing Demographic Shifts and the Impact on Market Share

In the dynamic and rapidly evolving global landscape, demographic shifts are reshaping the business world, making supplier diversity a crucial strategic move for corporations. The growing diversity among consumers is undeniable, and engaging with diverse suppliers provides a smart avenue to tap into emerging markets. Racial and ethnic minorities, along with other underrepresented groups, form a significant portion of the consumer base, and working with diverse suppliers enables corporations to cater to their unique needs and preferences, leading to increased market share.

According to a report by Pew Research Center,[7] six notable demographic trends are influencing both the United States and the global landscape. Topics discussed include the rise of Generation Z, the projected growth of Hispanics as the largest racial or ethnic minority group in the US electorate, and the evolving concept of the family in American society. These trends underscore the importance of fostering diversity and inclusivity within corporations to resonate with the changing preferences and needs of diverse consumers and employees.

Customers nowadays seek businesses that align with their values, and embracing diversity and inclusion is a major aspect. Collaborating with diverse suppliers not only demonstrates a commitment to these values but also enhances the brand image, fostering customer loyalty and further bolstering market share.

Beyond financial gains, diverse populations wield substantial buying power that continues to grow. Neglecting these demographics means missed opportunities for revenue generation. Engaging with diverse suppliers opens doors to new revenue streams, positioning corporations ahead of competitors.

Innovation and creativity are invaluable in the business realm, and diverse suppliers bring fresh perspectives and ideas to the table. Collaborating with them sparks innovation within corporations, leading to products and services that resonate with diverse audiences, providing a competitive edge.

Supporting diverse suppliers contributes to economic growth and job creation in local communities, making a positive impact on society. By nurturing diverse supplier partnerships, corporations not only thrive but also contribute to the welfare of the communities they

---

7   Anthony Cilluffo and D'Vera Cohn, "6 demographic trends shaping the U.S. and the world in 2019," Pew Research Center, April 11, 2019, www.pewresearch.org/short-reads/2019/04/11/6-demographic-trends-shaping-the-u-s-and-the-world-in-2019/.

serve. A resilient supply chain is paramount in times of uncertainty, and diverse suppliers offer alternative sources of goods and services, reducing risks associated with disruptions, creating a safety net for corporations.

Long-term partnerships with diverse suppliers foster trust and collaboration, leading to mutual growth and shared success, creating a win-win situation for both parties. Moreover, supplier diversity goes beyond a mere checkbox exercise; it exemplifies corporate values centered on DEI. It serves as a tangible manifestation of a corporation's commitment to these principles.

Considering the ongoing demographic shifts, supplier diversity is the key to adaptability and future-proofing business strategies. Embracing diverse suppliers enables corporations to stay ahead of the curve and capitalize on the endless opportunities that a diverse world presents.

In conclusion, supplier diversity is a game-changer for corporations, embracing the changing world, making a positive societal impact, and, most importantly, increasing market share. In today's fiercely competitive business landscape, supplier diversity is a strategic necessity that no corporation can afford to overlook.

Cost Savings and Increased Competition

In the fast-paced and competitive business world, cost-saving strategies are crucial for maintaining a strong bottom line without compromising quality. Enter supplier diversity programs—they are not merely about ticking diversity and inclusion boxes, but they can significantly impact cost savings through increased competition.

Expanding the pool of potential vendors by engaging with diverse suppliers opens up a world of possibilities and choices. With a diverse supplier base, you can leverage competitive bidding to your advantage. Suppliers will go the extra mile to offer the best deals, giving you the freedom to compare multiple offers, negotiate optimal terms, and select the supplier that provides the most value for your investment.

Not just that, working with diverse suppliers brings an infusion of innovation to your organization. Diverse backgrounds and experiences bring fresh ideas and creative solutions to the table, leading to greater efficiency and cost-effective processes that give your business a competitive edge. Furthermore, diverse supplier engagement also reduces risk by diversifying your supply chain. No longer relying solely on one supplier, you gain more resilience and preparedness to handle any potential challenges or disruptions.

The enthusiasm of diverse suppliers to prove themselves translates into competitive pricing, better terms, and cost benefits for your organization. They are eager to be your partner of choice, and this results in tangible cost savings for your company.

Building partnerships with diverse suppliers fosters a spirit of trust and collaboration. By having each other's back, operations run smoothly, productivity soars, and operational headaches decrease—a definite win-win scenario.

The MIT Sloan School of Management conducted research on the financial benefits of diverse supply chains, revealing that supplier diversity initiatives can significantly reduce the purchasing costs for buyers across various industries. The findings were published in the MIT Sloan Management Review, highlighting the tangible advantages of embracing supplier diversity.

The research provides concrete examples of major savings achieved in different sectors. For instance, the Virginia state government achieved an impressive 12 percent reduction in procurement expenditures, while the radio spectrum industry reaped a staggering

$45 million in savings. Similarly, the logging industry successfully reduced its expenditures by 10 percent. These cost-saving outcomes demonstrate the effectiveness of supplier diversity initiatives.[8]

The key driver behind these financial benefits is the increased competition fostered by supplier diversity programs. By promoting diversity among suppliers, larger and more established businesses are unable to rely solely on price-based strategies. As a result, the level of competition is heightened, leading to improved cost efficiencies for buyers.

In conclusion, the research from MIT Sloan emphasizes that supplier diversity is not just a symbolic gesture, but a strategic business decision that can deliver significant financial advantages. Companies that embrace supplier diversity can experience reduced costs, increased competition, and enhanced efficiency, positioning themselves for long-term success in today's dynamic business environment.

Engaging with diverse suppliers benefits not just your business but also the community. Supporting local businesses drives economic growth and contributes to the well-being of the communities you serve. This commitment to social responsibility resonates with customers, who value companies that genuinely care and embrace diversity and inclusion.

So, the evidence is irrefutable—supplier diversity programs go beyond being a mere checkbox exercise. They are a strategic and intelligent move that leads to substantial cost savings while promoting a culture of innovation, efficiency, and success. Supplier diversity is not just about embracing diversity; it's about fostering a dynamic and inclusive environment that propels your business forward and sets you apart from the competition.

---

8   Simha Mummalaneni and Jonathan Z. Zhang, "Maximizing the Benefits of B2B Supplier Diversification," MIT Sloan Management Review, June 30, 2020, www.sloan-review.mit.edu/article/maximizing-the-benefits-of-b2b-supplier-diversification/.

In conclusion, supplier diversity is not only a sound business practice but also an avenue for empowering underrepresented communities, driving economic growth, and enhancing your organization's reputation. By embracing diversity and inclusion, your company not only becomes more competitive but also creates a positive impact on society at large. It's a win-win situation that should be at the core of every forward-thinking business strategy. So, why wait? Embrace supplier diversity and watch your business flourish in the increasingly diverse and inclusive world of tomorrow.

Corporate Social Responsibility and Environmental, Social, and Governance

Corporate Social Responsibility (CSR) and Environmental, Social, and Governance (ESG) are not just buzzwords; they are the pillars that underpin a company's commitment to making a positive impact on society and fostering sustainable business practices.

Imagine CSR as the moral compass for companies, including yours. It's about more than just profits; it's about making a meaningful difference in the world around us. Through CSR, your organization can give back to local communities, uphold ethical practices, and protect our precious environment. It's about aligning your business values with actions that resonate with both customers and employees.

ESG serves as the robust framework supporting your journey toward responsible business practices. The "E" represents Environmental, and it's all about reducing your ecological footprint, promoting resource conservation, and contributing to a greener planet. The "S" stands for Social, emphasizing inclusivity, diversity, and treating people with fairness and respect across your supply chain. Lastly, the

"G" signifies Governance, ensuring ethical decision-making, transparency, and accountability within your organization.

I firmly believe that supplier diversity is an indispensable bridge that connects CSR and ESG with your business operations. It's about forging impactful partnerships with diverse suppliers, including minority-owned, women-owned, LGBTQ+, veteran-owned, and disability-owned businesses.

Supplier Diversity and the Environment

Supplier diversity programs extend their positive impact beyond just business benefits; they also contribute to a greener and more sustainable environment. By implementing supplier diversity strategies, corporations can foster environmentally friendly practices and play a role in shaping a greener future.

One of the key ways supplier diversity positively affects the environment is through local sourcing. Embracing supplier diversity often involves working with local businesses, which reduces transportation-related emissions and promotes a more environmentally friendly supply chain. By sourcing goods and services locally, companies can minimize their carbon footprint and support their local communities.

Additionally, diverse suppliers are often committed to eco-friendly practices. Many of these suppliers prioritize sustainability, renewable energy, and waste reduction in their operations. By collaborating with such suppliers, corporations can adopt and promote these eco-friendly practices within their own operations.

Moreover, diverse suppliers are known for their innovative ideas, which often include green innovations. Companies that partner with these suppliers gain access to cutting-edge green technologies and solutions, which can further contribute to sustainable business practices.

A crucial aspect of supplier diversity's positive environmental impact is the integration of environmental considerations into procurement decisions. By choosing suppliers with strong green practices, companies send a message to the entire supply chain about the importance of eco-consciousness. This ripple effect can encourage other businesses to adopt more sustainable practices as well.

Many diverse suppliers actively participate in the circular economy. They design products with a focus on reusability, remanufacturing, or recycling, reducing waste and contributing to a more sustainable world. By working with such suppliers, corporations can be part of a circular economy movement that aims to reduce resource consumption and waste generation.

In addition to eco-friendly practices, diverse suppliers often share their environmental knowledge and provide training to their corporate partners. This educational aspect enhances eco-awareness within the corporation and empowers employees to adopt sustainable practices in their daily work.

Furthermore, embracing supplier diversity and sustainable practices can enhance a company's reputation. Demonstrating commitment to the environment resonates with customers and stakeholders, building trust and loyalty. Companies that prioritize sustainability are often viewed as responsible and forward-thinking, which can positively impact their brand image and market perception.

Compliance with environmental laws and regulations is critical for businesses. Supplier diversity programs can help companies stay compliant with stringent environmental regulations, reducing the risk of penalties and fostering a culture of responsible business practices.

In conclusion, the business case for supplier diversity is undeniably strong and multifaceted. By embracing supplier diversity, corporations can reap numerous benefits that positively impact their bottom line and overall success.

First and foremost, supplier diversity programs align with CSR and ESG initiatives. They reflect a company's commitment to DEI, and demonstrate that the corporation is actively contributing to a more equitable and diverse business landscape.

Moreover, supplier diversity programs enable corporations to tap into emerging markets and reach diverse consumer populations. As demographic shifts continue to shape the global landscape, engaging with diverse suppliers becomes a strategic move to connect with a broader customer base and gain a competitive edge in the market.

The integration of diverse suppliers into a corporation's supply chain fosters innovation and creativity. These suppliers bring fresh perspectives and unique ideas, which can lead to the development of products and services that resonate with diverse audiences. Innovation drives efficiency and enhances a corporation's ability to meet customer needs effectively.

Supplier diversity also plays a significant role in fostering strong partnerships and collaboration. Developing relationships with diverse suppliers fosters trust, communication, and shared success. This collaborative approach to business enhances productivity and can lead to mutually beneficial opportunities for growth and innovation.

In addition to these business benefits, supplier diversity contributes to environmental sustainability. Embracing local sourcing and eco-friendly practices through diverse suppliers can help reduce a company's carbon footprint and support a greener supply chain. This commitment to environmental responsibility aligns with ESG goals and enhances a company's reputation as a socially conscious and responsible organization.

Furthermore, supplier diversity programs support economic growth and job creation within local communities. By engaging with diverse suppliers, corporations contribute to the economic empowerment of underrepresented groups, leading to broader economic development and prosperity.

In summary, supplier diversity is not just a checkbox exercise but a strategic move that offers tangible benefits. It strengthens a company's reputation, expands market share, fosters innovation, and promotes sustainability. Embracing supplier diversity is an investment in the future, signaling that a corporation is not only focused on short-term gains but also committed to making a positive impact on society and the environment. By embracing diversity and inclusion through supplier diversity programs, corporations can create a more equitable, sustainable, and prosperous business landscape for all.

For more information about how to measure the impact of supplier diversity programs, go to
https://jkasolutions.com/diversify&prosper.com

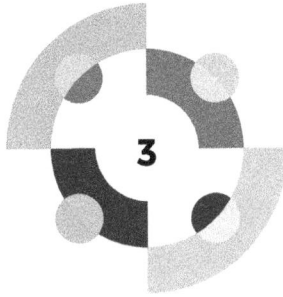

3

The Framework for a Sustainable Supplier Diversity Plan

When it comes to creating a successful and sustainable supplier diversity program, the commitment of senior leadership is paramount. We're not just talking about department heads here; we're talking about the board members and C-suite executives. Throughout this book, you'll find that we emphasize the importance of C-suite buy-in repeatedly, and that's because without it, the program's chances of success are greatly diminished.

Time and time again, we see companies attempting to implement supplier diversity programs in response to external pressures, such as community demands or government contract requirements. However, in these situations, when tough decisions must be made, supplier diversity goals often take a backseat to other objectives that hold more weight with board members and senior executives. For instance, a company culture solely focused on maximizing profits for shareholders might prioritize larger corporate purchases that neglect supplier diversity initiatives.

On the flip side, when supplier diversity goals are supported and sanctioned by senior leadership, it's a game-changer. You'll notice a clear shift in the organization's approach, with a genuine emphasis on corporate responsibility. This might manifest in providing updates and information about supplier diversity efforts and community engagement in the firm's annual report, demonstrating the commitment to transparency and accountability.

One crucial element in gaining and maintaining senior leadership's support is through meetings with key leadership members across various departments. It's essential to be open and transparent with them, sharing both successes and challenges. As you've defined your process, they'll have a better understanding of what to expect, and they'll be more likely to buy into the program.

If the leaders within an organization are truly invested in creating a sustainable supplier diversity program, they'll actively engage and support the efforts to address the complexities involved. Introducing new suppliers into an environment where they may not have been previously welcomed or where they lack experience and past performance can be a delicate process. It requires a significant shift in culture, policies, and procedures, and building trust takes time.

When seeking to garner support from senior leadership for your supplier diversity program, you must approach the matter with a well-structured and professional strategy. Effectively engaging senior leaders involves presenting a compelling business case that resonates with their objectives and values.

To begin, a data-driven approach is essential. Demonstrating the tangible benefits of supplier diversity through key performance indicators (KPIs) such as cost savings, revenue growth, and market expansion will capture their attention. Numbers speak volumes, and senior leaders are keen on seeing concrete evidence of how this initiative can enhance the company's financial performance.

However, it's not solely about financial gains. We must also emphasize the alignment between supplier diversity and our company's CSR goals. Highlighting how this program positively impacts society and fosters an inclusive corporate culture will showcase our commitment to making a meaningful difference.

A critical element in gaining their support is sharing successful case studies from other companies that have thrived through supplier diversity. These real-life examples will illustrate the program's potential and provide assurance that it has been proven effective in driving positive outcomes.

Moreover, we should actively involve senior leaders from the outset. Seeking their input and engagement in the program's design and implementation process will make them feel valued and invested in its success. Collaboration and open communication will reinforce the sense of a shared vision.

It is essential to address any concerns or skepticism head-on. By proactively addressing potential challenges and outlining mitigation strategies, we demonstrate our readiness to navigate obstacles with confidence.

Enlisting external expertise, such as industry thought leaders or subject matter experts, can also bolster our case. Their insights and support will lend credibility to our initiative and reinforce its significance in the broader business landscape.

Above all, we must emphasize that supplier diversity is not merely an ancillary initiative but a fundamental aspect of our strategic planning. By prioritizing it as a core element of our business strategy, we signal its importance to senior leadership and reinforce its enduring presence on the corporate agenda.

Lastly, recognizing and celebrating the accomplishments of diverse suppliers will reinforce the program's value and foster a culture of support and inclusion.

By adopting a well-informed, data-driven, and professionally presented approach, we can secure the buy-in and support of senior leadership for our supplier diversity program. Demonstrating the tangible benefits, aligning with CSR goals, and involving senior leaders from the beginning will solidify their commitment to this vital initiative. With a clear and compelling business case, we can propel our supplier diversity program to new heights and drive lasting positive impact.

CASE STUDY

Gaining Senior Leadership Buy-In for Supplier Diversity at ABC Corporation

Challenge

At ABC Corporation (a fake name I'm using as an example), we faced the challenge of getting senior leadership fully on board with the implementation of a supplier diversity program. The client's team exhibited reluctance and skepticism toward the idea, mainly due to concerns about the program's impact on costs and the perceived operational complexities. Overcoming these barriers and securing top-level support was crucial for the successful establishment of the supplier diversity initiative.

Strategies and Tactics

1. *Build a Compelling Business Case:* We began by developing a compelling business case that showcased the potential benefits of supplier diversity. Through extensive research and data analysis, we demonstrated how engaging with diverse suppliers could drive cost savings, boost market share, and foster innovation. Presenting this data-backed evidence to senior leadership helped them see the tangible value of the program and its positive impact on the company's bottom line.

2. *Align with Corporate Goals:* We emphasized how the supplier diversity initiative aligned with ABC Corporation's overarching corporate goals and values. By linking supplier diversity to the company's mission and strategic objectives, we highlighted how the initiative could enhance the company's reputation as a socially responsible organization committed to diversity and inclusion.

3. *Tackle Concerns Head-On:* To address the team's concerns, we facilitated open and honest discussions with senior leadership. We listened to their apprehensions and provided transparent answers, debunking myths about potential costs and complexities. By assuaging their fears, we built trust and credibility, showing that supplier diversity was not a burden, but an opportunity for growth.

4. *Showcase Success Stories:* We shared success stories from our other clients that had successfully implemented supplier

diversity programs. These case studies demonstrated how embracing diversity had positively impacted their businesses and helped create a more inclusive and innovative supply chain. Real-life examples were powerful in illustrating the potential of supplier diversity to senior leadership.

5. *Establish Metrics and Performance Goals:* To instill accountability, we recommended setting clear metrics and performance goals for the supplier diversity program. By tying these goals to KPIs, we made it evident that the program's success would be monitored and reported at the senior leadership level. This approach encouraged their active involvement and commitment.

6. *Leverage External Support:* To reinforce the importance of supplier diversity, we enlisted external support from industry experts and diversity advocates. Engaging guest speakers and experts to present the benefits of supplier diversity further emphasized its significance and lent credibility to the initiative.

Results

By leveraging these strategies and tactics, we successfully garnered buy-in from senior leadership at ABC Corporation. The compelling business case, alignment with corporate goals, and transparent communication addressed their concerns and led to a shift in their perception of supplier diversity.

The establishment of clear metrics and performance goals provided a sense of direction and accountability, ensuring that senior leadership actively championed the initiative. The use of success stories and external support further reinforced the potential impact of supplier diversity, inspiring leaders to support the initiative wholeheartedly.

Conclusion

Obtaining senior leadership buy-in for a supplier diversity program requires a combination of compelling arguments, transparent communication, and a focus on alignment with corporate goals. By addressing concerns, showcasing success stories, and providing external support, we were able to secure the commitment of senior leadership at ABC Corporation. This case study exemplifies the importance of persistence, strategic planning, and open dialogue in navigating resistance and building support for supplier diversity initiatives at the highest level of the organization.

Data Management and Analysis

When considering the implementation of a supplier diversity program, one essential factor to prioritize is data. Data plays a pivotal role in supporting KPIs and ensuring the success of your program. It should be integrated into the program's framework from the start to establish a strong foundation.

An important aspect of this process involves effectively tracking and managing data and information. It requires careful thought and planning to determine the responsible individuals or teams, the storage and accessibility of the data, and the regular updating procedures. The availability of comprehensive and up-to-date data is crucial in developing a robust system that can be maintained over time. The significance of data cannot be overstated in this context.

By giving due attention to data management within your supplier diversity program, you lay the groundwork for success. It empowers you to make informed decisions, assess progress, identify areas for improvement, and showcase the impact of your supplier diversity efforts. Ultimately, the quality and accessibility of data play a vital role in building and sustaining an effective supplier diversity program.

A well-rounded supplier diversity program relies on comprehensive data, including information about the types of goods and services procured and their corresponding values. It is essential to analyze not only the quantity and frequency of purchases but also the monetary significance attached to them.

Additionally, exploration of existing contract values and their expiration dates is a crucial aspect of this data set. Understanding the contractual landscape provides insights into the longevity and stability of your supplier relationships. It allows you to identify upcoming contract renewals or terminations, which presents opportunities to incorporate supplier diversity considerations during the contract renegotiation process.

By examining the types of goods and services purchased, as well as their corresponding values, you can gain a holistic view of your organization's procurement practices. This comprehensive understanding enables you to identify areas where supplier diversity can be enhanced, such as by actively seeking diverse suppliers for high-value purchases or strategically incorporating supplier diversity requirements into upcoming contract negotiations.

Analyzing contract values and expiration dates provides a proactive approach to managing your supplier diversity program. It allows you to plan ahead, ensuring that supplier diversity considerations are integrated into your organization's procurement strategy and decision-making processes.

By leveraging this valuable data, you can foster a more inclusive and diverse supplier base while maximizing the value and impact of your organization's procurement efforts.

As you delve deeper into the analysis of purchasing patterns and vendor demographics, noteworthy trends begin to emerge. These findings serve as foundational pillars for a supplier diversity program, guiding strategic actions and initiatives.

By closely examining the composition of expenditures, valuable insights can be gained into the allocation of financial resources. This enables organizations to identify potential opportunities for enhancing supplier diversity. For instance, significant expenditures in technology or professional services may warrant proactive efforts to seek out diverse suppliers within those categories, fostering greater inclusivity.

Simultaneously, understanding the composition of the vendor pool provides a comprehensive view of the current supplier diversity landscape. It sheds light on the representation of diverse businesses within the supply chain and helps gauge the extent of inclusivity achieved thus far. Connecting the dots between procurement patterns and vendor demographics uncovers compelling trends that influence the strategic approach. For example, a concentration of women-owned businesses in a specific category may present a unique opportunity to amplify support for these suppliers and foster diversity within that particular realm.

Another interesting thing you can do with all that data is figure out who your top ten suppliers are. Take a look at what makes them successful. Then reach out to each one and ask them if they have a supplier diversity program in place. If they do, then ask them about it. What pitfalls have they encountered? What policies and procedures do they have in place? The good, bad, and the ugly of it all. You can then use that information to learn from their mistakes and successes and put together a very inclusive system.

Another important aspect of establishing a supplier diversity program is understanding the availability of qualified suppliers by partnering with state and local organizations. These collaborations play a crucial role in gaining insights into the supplier landscape and identifying vendors who meet diversity and inclusion criteria.

State and local organizations offer valuable resources and expertise to help identify and evaluate diverse suppliers. They provide access to databases, certifications, and directories that feature qualified businesses from various underrepresented groups, including minorities, women, veterans, and more. By leveraging these partnerships, businesses can ensure a comprehensive pool of diverse suppliers is considered for their procurement needs.

Engaging with state and local organizations allows businesses to tap into their knowledge and networks. These organizations possess deep insights into the local business ecosystem and can identify emerging diverse suppliers who may not be widely known. They also offer guidance on certification processes, training opportunities, and business development support, facilitating the growth and success of diverse suppliers within the supply chain.

Here are a few examples of organizations that can play a pivotal role:

1. *Minority Business Development Agencies (MBDAs):* These organizations focus on promoting the growth and development of minority-owned businesses within their respective states. They provide resources, certifications, and networking opportunities to connect diverse suppliers with corporate partners.

2. *Local Chambers of Commerce:* Chambers of commerce at the local level actively support and advocate for businesses in their communities. They often have dedicated initiatives to promote supplier diversity and can facilitate connections between local diverse suppliers and corporations.

3. *National Minority Supplier Development Council:* As one of the leading organizations in supplier diversity, NMSDC certifies and connects minority-owned businesses with corporate members. Their extensive network spans across industries and regions, providing access to a wide range of diverse suppliers.

4. *Women's Business Enterprise National Council:* WBENC is dedicated to advancing women-owned businesses through certification and supplier diversity programs. They offer resources and connections for corporations seeking to engage with women-owned suppliers.

5. *National LGBT Chamber of Commerce (NGLCC):* NGLCC promotes economic opportunities and supplier diversity for lesbian, gay, bisexual, and transgender (LGBT)-owned businesses. Their certification and networking programs facilitate partnerships between corporations and LGBT-owned suppliers.

Data is essential for addressing challenges that arise when corporations prioritize supply chain efficiency and cost-effectiveness. It helps make the business case for allocating a portion of spending toward diverse suppliers.

Having the right data set is crucial when it comes to challenging established mindsets in procurement teams and supply chains. While changing these mindsets overnight may not be feasible, data can be a powerful tool to influence perceptions and drive positive change. By leveraging compelling data that demonstrates the benefits of supplier diversity, such as increased market share and improved business performance, you can gradually shift the mindset within your organization. The data serves as evidence, allowing you to effectively make the case for embracing supplier diversity and breaking away from traditional practices. Over time, as decision-makers see the tangible impact and potential growth opportunities associated with supplier diversity, their mindset can evolve, paving the way for a more inclusive and progressive approach to procurement.

Once you have established a solid framework for your supplier diversity program, it becomes a valuable tool in your decision-making process. The data you analyze not only provides insights for immediate actions but also helps identify trends over longer periods. By extending your analysis beyond a few years, you can uncover valuable patterns that might have gone unnoticed. For instance, during challenging economic times, your company may naturally lean toward local suppliers more frequently. Alternatively, you might have initially worked with diverse suppliers but gradually shifted away from them as your company grew. By examining these trends, you gain valuable insights that guide your future actions and allow you to make informed decisions. The data becomes your ally, providing guidance on what strategies to pursue and what to avoid, ultimately contributing to the success and effectiveness of your supplier diversity program.

With all of this information in hand, you can start thinking about goals and metrics. It could be a percentage of overall purchases being from diverse suppliers. Then you can break that goal down even further and start thinking about it from local, regional, and national levels.

This may seem like a lot of work, but there is a method to this madness. The data you glean from this process will show you interesting things. Certain firms, industries, and services will cluster in specific regions. There may be more construction in one town that's booming, while two counties over they have other services on hand. By knowing who is in your market and understanding industry trends, your program is more likely to succeed.

Local politics can play a significant role in the implementation of supplier diversity programs. As businesses expand their operations across different states or cities, they may encounter varying political climates and regulations that impact the promotion of supplier diversity. Navigating these political landscapes becomes essential to ensure smooth program execution and compliance with local requirements.

Economics also come into play when considering supplier diversity. Evaluating the cost-effectiveness of shipping goods from distant locations versus sourcing them locally becomes a crucial decision-making factor. While supporting local businesses fosters community development and reduces environmental impact, affordability and logistics must be carefully assessed to strike the right balance.

In a nutshell, data analysis is the superhero of supplier diversity programs. It's the secret sauce that makes the whole thing tick. By integrating data right from the get-go and managing it like a pro, you gain the power to make smart decisions, track progress, and spot opportunities for improvement.

And let me tell you, having up-to-date data is like having a magic crystal ball. It shows you trends over time, uncovers valuable patterns, and helps you plan for the future. You can see how your spending habits change during tough times, or how you might've drifted away from diverse suppliers as your company grew.

But that's not all. Data opens up a treasure trove of supplier insights. You can identify your top suppliers, pick their brains about their diversity programs (the good, the bad, and the ugly), and learn from their experiences.

Procurement

Let us now look into the captivating world of procurement strategy. I affectionately refer to it as the "deep dive on procurement," and believe me, you can effortlessly adopt this approach, too. The method empowers you with incredibly robust data.

As a starting point, meticulously gather information on all purchase activities from the past three years. This process lays the foundation for your procurement expedition, unveiling a plethora of opportunities waiting to be explored. Simultaneously, it stimulates decision-makers within your organization to contemplate potential areas for outsourcing.

When diving into your three years of purchasing data, it's crucial to identify significant trends, including a focus on purchases from local suppliers. Take note of whether you are consistently buying from the same vendors and the specific characteristics that define these relationships. However, don't limit your analysis to just formal procurement transactions. Extend it to encompass smaller types of purchases, such as consulting services, event planning, and office supplies, which may involve local suppliers. This comprehensive examination will provide valuable insights into your organization's spending patterns and the impact of local supplier relationships on your overall procurement strategy.

Once you've examined your local and diverse supplier purchases—both tracked and untracked—you'll discover valuable contacts scattered throughout your organization. Those seemingly small ad hoc purchases add up, trust me.

As we embark on the exciting quest of increasing spending with diverse suppliers, I can't stress enough the significance of historical data. It serves as a vital compass, guiding us by illuminating where we've come from and where we can head next. For instance, if we've been dedicating 10 percent of the budget to local and diverse suppliers in the past, it provides a solid starting point to build upon.

One crucial aspect we mustn't overlook during the data analysis is the influence of volume discounts and incentives offered by larger suppliers. These factors might not be immediately apparent in our budget, but they can significantly impact our supplier diversity efforts. It's essential to understand how volume discounts work and the incentives that larger suppliers may provide based on the scale of our purchases. While these deals can offer cost savings, we should also be mindful of their potential effects on our efforts to foster a sustainable supplier diversity program.

As we explore our spending patterns and assess potential suppliers, let's keep a keen eye on these dynamics. The goal is to strike the right balance between maximizing cost-effectiveness and ensuring we create opportunities for local and diverse suppliers.

By raising awareness about the existence and impact of volume discounts and incentives, we can make informed decisions that align with our commitment to supplier diversity. So, as we move forward, let's be proactive in considering these factors and create a robust strategy that propels us toward a more inclusive and successful procurement approach.

Sometimes, you'll bump into specific policies that push for cost efficiency. The buyers are incentivized to save money and receive bonuses based on their savings. Now how do you work through this?

Well, reviewing policies and procedures becomes critical. Address any friction points before you proceed to ensure the success of your program.

In the end, it's all about seizing opportunities. Analyze your data, strategize, and counter any debate with solid arguments. Whether it's economic impact analysis or the perks of local suppliers, you'll demonstrate the value of supplier diversity.

Navigating change can be challenging, especially for larger organizations, but a well-communicated plan and data-backed decisions pave the way for a sustainable program.

So there you have it: A treasure trove of data awaits you on this journey. Get ready to wield its power and transform your procurement process like a pro.

Identifying and Overcoming Obstacles

Implementing a supplier diversity program in a large corporation is no simple task, and it comes with its fair share of barriers to overcome. Let's take a closer look at the key challenges we may encounter.

When it comes to championing supplier diversity, I won't sugarcoat it—it's no walk in the park. There are hurdles and road-blocks that we must be prepared to face head-on. Let's head into some of the key barriers to success, drawing inspiration from real-world examples and insights from industry experts.

INTERNAL RESISTANCE: "THE ELEPHANT IN THE ROOM"

Picture this: You're all fired up, ready to revolutionize your organization with a robust supplier diversity program. But then, boom! You're met with resistance from within—hesitant stakeholders who cling to the status quo like their lives depend on it.

It's like trying to move an elephant in a crowded room—a monumental challenge. But fear not, this is an all-too-common barrier that many diversity champions encounter. In my own experience working with a large corporation seeking to enhance their supplier diversity, I witnessed internal resistance from some key decision-makers. Their apprehensions stemmed from concerns about potential disruptions in supply chains, perceived higher costs associated with diverse suppliers, and a general reluctance to deviate from established procurement practices. To address this resistance, we embarked on a comprehensive engagement campaign, sharing success stories from other companies that had successfully implemented supplier diversity programs. We also organized workshops and training sessions to educate stakeholders about the tangible benefits of a diverse supplier pool, including greater innovation, improved market responsiveness, and enhanced brand reputation.

DATA DILEMMAS: UNRAVELING THE DIVERSITY PUZZLE

Ah, data. The backbone of any successful endeavor. Yet, in the context of supplier diversity, data can be a tricky beast to tame. Incomplete or inaccurate data can cripple our efforts to set meaningful goals and measure progress effectively.

That's where meticulous data management comes in. I recall reading a piece on supplier diversity data management by Supply Chain Dive, highlighting the significance of investing in robust systems and processes to ensure we have a solid grip on the diversity puzzle.

I encountered significant data challenges in one of my projects. The organization had historical spending data scattered across various departments, and it was a herculean task to consolidate and cleanse the information to derive actionable insights. To address this barrier, we enlisted the expertise of data analysts and leveraged advanced analytics tools to collate, cleanse, and analyze the data comprehensively. Armed with accurate and detailed supplier spending information, we were better equipped to identify opportunities for increased spending with diverse suppliers and demonstrate the economic impact of our program.

THE "UNICORN" SEARCH: QUALIFIED DIVERSE SUPPLIERS

Seeking qualified diverse suppliers can be like searching for unicorns: rare and seemingly mythical creatures. In certain industries, finding businesses that tick all the diversity boxes can be quite the challenge. To be clear, it's not because they don't exist, it's more about the process for engaging with diverse suppliers.

In a manufacturing company's journey to bolster their supplier diversity, they faced the barrier of limited qualified diverse suppliers in their industry. They tackled this challenge by partnering with local business organizations, trade associations, and supplier diversity councils to identify and develop potential suppliers from underrepresented groups. Additionally, they initiated outreach programs to connect with diverse entrepreneurs and create mentorship opportunities to help them navigate the complexities of supply chains. By actively cultivating and supporting diverse suppliers, they built a diverse network that added value not only to their own business but also to their local community.

COMPLEX ONBOARDING: A DETRIMENT TO DIVERSE SUPPLIERS

Picture yourself navigating a labyrinthine maze just to qualify as a vendor. Well, that's the reality for many diverse suppliers facing overly complicated vendor qualification processes. This complexity can deter diverse businesses from participating, hurting both them and our mission.

Simplifying and streamlining onboarding procedures should be a priority.

In a case study involving a financial institution, they recognized that their lengthy and cumbersome vendor qualification process was deterring diverse suppliers from even attempting to participate. They took a proactive approach to streamline the process, removing unnecessary red tape and simplifying requirements without compromising on compliance or quality. Additionally, they invested in training and support for diverse suppliers to guide them through the onboarding process, ensuring that qualified businesses could easily become part of the supplier pool. As a result, the organization saw a notable increase in diverse supplier participation and, ultimately, supplier diversity success.

THE CRYSTAL-CLEAR VISION: DEFINING PROGRAM GOALS

Ah, the quintessential "vision quest." Without well-defined and measurable program goals, we're navigating in the dark without a flashlight. Setting clear objectives is fundamental to the success of any supplier diversity initiative.

In my own experience working with a technology company, they initially struggled with their supplier diversity program due to a lack of clearly defined goals. They set out on a journey of internal discovery, engaging key stakeholders to align on the program's vision, mission, and specific objectives. By conducting workshops and strategy sessions, they co-created a clear road map with well-defined targets, such as increasing spending with diverse suppliers by a certain percentage each year and fostering supplier development initiatives. With a united front and a crystal-clear vision, the organization saw increased support from both employees and suppliers, resulting in a more successful supplier diversity program.

Establish Reasonable Goals

So how do you define success for your new program? What targets do you want or need to hit, and what results will you see? By defining success early on, you will have a marker for where you need to hit, and that is important. Without those benchmarks, you could just keep hustling indefinitely trying to find a path that gets you to a non-existent finish line, and that's no fun for anybody.

Alright, let's talk about defining success for our supplier diversity program. It's like charting a course for an exciting adventure: you need a clear destination, a sense of direction, and a way to measure your progress. Without those markers, we'd be wandering aimlessly in uncharted waters, and that's no fun for anyone.

So, how do we set ourselves up for success? First things first, we need to establish well-defined goals and benchmarks. That's the compass that'll guide us through this journey and help us navigate any challenges that come our way.

Setting reasonable and achievable goals is the key here. We don't want to reach for the stars and end up disappointed. Instead, let's aim for targets that we can realistically hit, and that'll keep us motivated to push forward.

WHAT CAN WE MEASURE?

There are a few areas where we can set measurable goals for our supplier diversity program:

1. *Increasing Diverse Supplier Spend:* Let's put our money where our mouth is. We can set a goal to allocate a certain percentage of our spending to diverse suppliers. For instance, companies like The Walt Disney Company and Accenture have set targets to spend a certain amount with diverse suppliers, and they've achieved impressive results.

2. *Expanding Our Diverse Supplier Base:* We want to widen the pool of qualified diverse suppliers we work with. By nurturing and developing a diverse supplier ecosystem, we create opportunities for more businesses to thrive. General Motors' "Mentor–Protégé Program" is a great example of how this approach can lead to growth and success for diverse suppliers.

3. *Fostering Supplier Diversity across Categories:* It's not just about diversifying spending. We can aim to have a diverse supply chain in different business categories. For instance, companies like Intel have set goals to achieve 100 percent diversity in categories like manufacturing and construction.

The Positive Impact of Supplier Diversity

A supplier diversity program shouldn't be a checkbox exercise; it can have a profound impact on various aspects of your corporation and the community. Here are some of the positive outcomes we can look forward to:

1. *Community Growth and Economic Impact:* When we engage with diverse suppliers, we're contributing to the local economy. Studies show that for every $1 million in revenue generated by diverse suppliers, around seventeen jobs are created within the community. It's a win-win situation for everyone involved.

2. *Brand Reputation and Public Relations:* Commitment to supplier diversity can be a powerful PR tool. Customers and stakeholders appreciate businesses that value inclusivity. Companies like Johnson & Johnson have successfully showcased their supplier diversity efforts through campaigns, enhancing their brand image.

3. *Innovation and Fresh Perspectives:* Diverse suppliers bring unique perspectives and innovative solutions to the table. It goes without saying that diversity of thought enhances innovation.

4. *Regulatory Compliance and Corporate Responsibility:* For some industries, supplier diversity is not just a nice-to-have; it's a must-have. It aligns with regulatory requirements and demonstrates our commitment to CSR.

5. *Business Resilience and Risk Mitigation:* Diversifying our supply chain can minimize risk during disruptions. The COVID-19 pandemic highlighted the importance of having multiple suppliers to ensure business continuity.

A Journey Toward Inclusion

In this supplier diversity journey, success isn't just about reaching a destination. It's about the positive impact we create along the way. The measurable goals we set will guide us, keep us focused, and remind us of the progress we're making.

Remember, it's not just about hitting targets; it's about building a better future for everyone involved. So let's set sail with confidence, embrace diversity, and make a real difference in our organization, community, and beyond.

You have to define success so you know when you reach it. Then you have to think about the goals for the program. You know what it takes to succeed, but how are you going to get there? I've gone through this process with several clients and can share some case studies below.

CASE STUDY

Empowering Supplier Diversity in the Healthcare Industry

In the ever-evolving landscape of the healthcare industry, supplier diversity has emerged as a powerful tool to drive innovation, enhance patient care, and strengthen community engagement. This case study delves into the transformative journey undertaken by a leading healthcare organization, referred to here as "HealthFirst Medical Systems," to harness the potential of supplier diversity and create a lasting impact in their organization and the communities they serve.

Goal 1: Hardwiring Supplier Diversity into the Organization's DNA

Policies, Procedures, and Practices Overhaul

To kickstart their supplier diversity program, HealthFirst recognized the need for a holistic approach. Collaborating with our team of experts, they embarked on an in-depth analysis of their existing policies, procedures, and practices. This led to a comprehensive overhaul to ensure that supplier diversity was seamlessly integrated into their core values and daily operations.

Example: A notable recommendation included revising their sourcing policies to mandate that a certain percentage of contracts must be awarded to diverse suppliers. This strategic shift served as a tangible testament to HealthFirst's commitment to supplier diversity.

Measuring Success with KPIs

HealthFirst understood the importance of quantifiable metrics in assessing the impact of their efforts. KPIs were carefully crafted to measure progress and outcomes related to supplier diversity.

Example: A vital KPI focused on increasing the percentage of spending with diverse suppliers compared to previous years. This target incentivized the procurement team to actively seek out certified diverse businesses and establish mutually beneficial partnerships.

Empowering the Procurement Team

Recognizing that people drive change, HealthFirst invested in empowering their procurement professionals to become champions of diversity. JKA developed a comprehensive training regimen to equip them with the knowledge and tools needed to embrace supplier diversity wholeheartedly.

Example: The procurement team received a supplier diversity training manual that offered insights into the value of supplier diversity and practical strategies to identify and engage with diverse suppliers. Additionally, a tool kit was designed to streamline the procurement process, ensuring diversity considerations remained a priority.

Goal 2: Expanding Spending with Diverse and Local Suppliers

Strategic Outreach Initiatives

HealthFirst was dedicated to broadening their supplier base to include diverse and local businesses. We worked closely with them to design a strategic outreach strategy that would create a more robust and inclusive supplier network.

Example: A significant initiative involved hosting a Diverse Supplier Expo, where certified diverse businesses were invited to showcase their offerings and directly connect with HealthFirst's procurement team. This event not only opened doors to exciting new partnerships but also nurtured a culture of inclusivity within the organization.

Enhancing Supplier Evaluation Tools

Realizing that evaluation is crucial in making informed decisions, HealthFirst introduced tools that went beyond traditional metrics. They considered factors like innovation, environmental sustainability, and community impact in their supplier evaluation process.

Example: The Supplier Diversity Scorecard emerged as a game-changer. By assessing suppliers holistically, it allowed HealthFirst to select partners aligned with their values and mission, fostering a ripple effect of positive change.

Goal 3: Building Community Partnerships for Empowerment

Access to Capital and Mentorship

HealthFirst recognized the potential for supplier diversity to drive economic empowerment in their local communities. They collaborated with local banks and forged community partnerships that provided access to capital and mentorship opportunities for socially and economically disadvantaged businesses.

Example: HealthFirst partnered with local community development financial institutions (CDFIs) to offer favorable financing options to diverse suppliers. This initiative enabled small businesses to grow and thrive, contributing to a more vibrant and inclusive local economy.

Mentoring and Networking Opportunities

The journey to success often benefits from guidance and support. HealthFirst instituted mentorship and networking programs that connected diverse suppliers with established industry leaders.

Example: Quarterly networking events facilitated meaningful connections between diverse suppliers and key decision-makers within HealthFirst. These connections not only increased contract opportunities but also nurtured a supportive and collaborative business environment.

Conclusion

HealthFirst Medical System's commitment to supplier diversity serves as an inspiring case study, highlighting the transformative power of inclusion within the healthcare industry. By hardwiring supplier diversity into their core values, enhancing procurement practices, and expanding spending with diverse and local suppliers, HealthFirst has emerged as a beacon of innovation and community empowerment. Their journey showcases how a purpose-driven supplier diversity program not only enriches an organization's supply chain but also fosters positive change that reaches far beyond its walls. As we continue to witness the success and impact of HealthFirst's supplier diversity program, it stands as a testament to the tremendous possibilities that unfold when diversity becomes a driving force in healthcare procurement.

The concept of goal setting is nothing new, but it is often misunderstood. People will say, "I want to buy a bigger house," but then have no plan on how to execute. Your goals need to have that execution component in there.

One way to do that is with SMART goals. If you have been in the corporate world for any period of time, chances are you have already heard of these. The concept is to create a goal that meets the criteria laid out in the acronym: Specific, Measurable, Achievable, Relevant, and Time-Bound. The easiest way to do this is by laying out each letter of the acronym and answering them. There are entire books dedicated to the concept of SMART goals, but you get the idea. If you make your goals clear, then they can easily turn into reality. Here is another example of work we did with a construction client.

CASE STUDY

Empowering Supplier Diversity Through SMART Goals

In this case study, we dive into the journey of a construction company, ConstructionCo, as they sought to create a robust and impactful supplier diversity program. Their aspirations were clear: they wanted to promote diversity in their supply chain while fostering inclusive growth in the communities they served. However, like many organizations, they faced challenges in translating this vision into actionable plans. The key was to adopt

SMART goals to drive meaningful progress and maximize the positive impact of their supplier diversity program.

The Challenge: Translating Aspirations into Concrete Actions

ConstructionCo recognized the need for a more diverse supplier base to enrich their business ecosystem and reflect the diverse communities they served. However, they struggled to make their supplier diversity program a reality. They lacked a structured approach to set achievable goals and measure success effectively. Their efforts needed direction and a well-defined path to make a tangible impact on supplier diversity.

The SMART Solution

ConstructionCo decided to adopt SMART goals, providing a strategic framework to make their supplier diversity program a success. Let's explore how each element of the acronym contributed to their journey:

1. Specific

ConstructionCo began by setting specific and well-defined goals for their supplier diversity program. Rather than a vague desire for "increased supplier diversity," they aimed to "increase the percentage of certified diverse suppliers in their procurement process by 15 percent within the next year."

2. Measurable

To track their progress, ConstructionCo incorporated measurable metrics into their supplier diversity goals. They established KPIs to evaluate outcomes, such as "conduct quarterly assessments of supplier diversity spend" and "monitor the number of diverse suppliers in each procurement category."

3. Achievable

ConstructionCo understood that their goals needed to be challenging yet realistic. They assessed their existing supplier base and identified potential diverse suppliers within their industry. This approach ensured they set achievable objectives, such as "increase the utilization of diverse suppliers in direct spend categories by 10 percent in the next six months."

4. Relevant

The goals ConstructionCo set for their supplier diversity program were directly aligned with their vision of fostering inclusion and creating a positive social impact. They aspired to "establish partnerships with local community organizations that support diverse businesses" to ensure their supplier diversity efforts were relevant and impactful.

5. Time-Bound

To instill a sense of urgency and accountability, ConstructionCo attached time-bound deadlines to their supplier diversity goals. For example, they set a target to "achieve a supplier diversity spend of 15 percent of the total procurement spend by the end of the fiscal year."

Illustrative Examples

SMART Goal: Enhancing Diverse Supplier Outreach

- *Specific:* Identify and engage with at least five new certified diverse suppliers from underrepresented communities in the next quarter.
- *Measurable:* Maintain a record of new diverse supplier partnerships and track their contributions to procurement spend.
- *Achievable:* Allocate resources to build a comprehensive outreach strategy and participate in supplier diversity events.
- *Relevant:* Strengthen the company's commitment to supplier diversity and support underrepresented businesses.
- *Time-Bound:* Achieve the goal of partnering with five new diverse suppliers by the end of Q3 2023.

SMART Goal: Increasing Diverse Supplier Spend

- *Specific:* Raise the percentage of direct spending with certified diverse suppliers to 20 percent within the next two fiscal quarters.
- *Measurable:* Monitor the percentage of diverse supplier spend regularly and report progress to stakeholders.
- *Achievable:* Analyze procurement data to identify areas where increased diverse supplier utilization is feasible.
- *Relevant:* Strengthen the supplier diversity program's impact on the community and contribute to inclusive growth.
- *Time-Bound:* Achieve the goal of 20 percent diverse supplier

spend by the end of the second fiscal quarter of 2024.

Conclusion

By incorporating SMART goals into their supplier diversity program, ConstructionCo transformed aspirations into tangible actions. The specific, measurable, achievable, relevant, and time-bound nature of their goals empowered them to track progress effectively, make data-driven decisions, and foster inclusion within their supply chain. Through this case study, we witness the power of SMART goals in propelling organizations toward achieving meaningful supplier diversity milestones, driving sustainable growth, and making a positive social impact in their industry and communities.

Establishing goals for a supplier diversity program can be difficult. I was working with a client who was worried about implementing a supplier diversity program because they didn't want retaliation. The concern was if they put a program in place, people would naturally ask what the client did previously. They were very concerned about what kinds of reactions they were going to face if they made their information public, because the truth of the matter was, they only had marginal success with their supplier diversity programs in the past. They didn't want to be judged for previous mistakes, which meant that if they kept with the status quo, nobody would be the wiser. Here is another case study highlighting some of the actions we took.

CASE STUDY

Overcoming Concerns and Building an Effective Supplier Diversity Program

Challenge

ABC Corporation was hesitant to implement a supplier diversity program due to concerns about potential retaliation and scrutiny from stakeholders. The client had experienced only marginal success with previous supplier diversity initiatives, and they were worried that past shortcomings might be used against them if they made their efforts public. They sought a strategy to address these concerns while establishing a robust and effective supplier diversity program.

Solution

1. *Developing an Effective Communication Plan:* We recognized that transparent communication would be key to addressing the client's concerns. To mitigate potential backlash, we developed a comprehensive communication plan that highlighted the company's commitment to diversity and inclusion. The plan emphasized the positive impact of supplier diversity on local communities and the overall business ecosystem.

   The communication plan outlined the steps ABC Corporation would take to improve its supplier diversity initiatives and showcased the potential benefits for all stakeholders involved. By being proactive in their communication efforts, the client aimed to gain support and understanding from employees, customers, and partners.

2. *Partnering with Local Community Members:* To build trust and demonstrate their genuine commitment to supplier diversity, ABC Corporation decided to engage with local community members and key stakeholders. We facilitated town hall meetings, focus groups, and one-on-one discussions to listen to the concerns and suggestions of community representatives. By involving the community in the decision-making process, ABC Corporation gained valuable insights into the specific needs and preferences of local businesses. This collaborative approach helped foster a sense of ownership and buy-in from the community, making it more likely for the supplier diversity program to be accepted and embraced.

3. *Setting Realistic Goals and Commitments:* To address the fear of potential scrutiny for past shortcomings, we advised ABC Corporation to set realistic and achievable goals for their supplier diversity program. Rather than making grandiose promises, we encouraged the client to take a data-driven approach and establish attainable milestones.

By setting incremental goals and commitments, ABC Corporation demonstrated a genuine dedication to continuous improvement. This approach allowed them to focus on tangible progress while avoiding overpromising and underdelivering, which could have led to negative perceptions.

Results

Through our strategic approach, ABC Corporation success-fully addressed their concerns and launched an effective supplier diversity program. The comprehensive communication plan provided stakeholders with a clear understanding of the company's intentions and commitment to diversity and inclusion.

By engaging with local community members, ABC Corporation gained valuable support and constructive feedback. This collaborative effort not only enhanced the credibility of their supplier diversity program but also strengthened their relationship with the community.

Setting realistic and achievable goals allowed ABC Corporation to demonstrate transparency and a commitment to progress. As a result, they received positive feedback from employees, customers, and partners, who appreciated the client's genuine efforts to foster a more diverse and inclusive supply chain.

Conclusion

The case of ABC Corporation demonstrates the importance of addressing concerns and building trust when implementing a supplier diversity program. By developing an effective communication plan, partnering with local community members, and setting realistic goals, the client successfully navigated potential challenges and launched a supplier diversity program that aligned with their corporate values.

Taking a proactive and collaborative approach to supplier diversity can lead to positive outcomes, fostering a culture of inclusivity, and driving meaningful change both within the company and the broader community. With a strong commitment to diversity and inclusion, ABC Corporation is well-positioned to create a more sustainable and equitable business environment while making a positive impact on society.

Putting the Pieces Together

As we navigate the path toward implementing a successful supplier diversity program, three critical pillars emerge: data management, overcoming barriers to success, and establishing sustainable goals. Through my experience and the case studies shared, it is evident that a well-executed supplier diversity program can have a transformative impact on an organization, its suppliers, and the communities it serves.

Data management forms the bedrock of any supplier diversity initiative. Understanding spending patterns, identifying potential diverse suppliers, and tracking progress are all contingent on the availability and accuracy of data. Therefore, investing in robust data management systems and processes is essential. By analyzing purchasing patterns and vendor characteristics over time, we can discern trends, identify opportunities, and ensure continuous improvement.

In the pursuit of supplier diversity, it is vital to address potential barriers to success head-on. Whether it's resistance from internal stakeholders, concerns about retaliation, or the challenge of incorporating diverse suppliers into existing procurement practices, each barrier requires careful consideration and strategic planning. Creating a safe space for open discussions, engaging leadership support, and involving key stakeholders facilitate smoother implementation. By reevaluating policies and practices and fostering cross-functional collaboration, we can mitigate potential roadblocks.

Establishing sustainable goals lies at the heart of a successful supplier diversity program. SMART goals—Specific, Measurable, Achievable, Relevant, and Time-Bound—provide a clear road map for progress. Aligning these goals with the organization's core values and corporate strategy ensures that supplier diversity becomes an integral part of the company's identity. Furthermore, defining your KPIs helps measure outcomes, track progress, and demonstrate the program's effectiveness.

A case study in the healthcare industry highlighted the importance of setting reasonable goals. By incorporating SMART goals, the company successfully increased spend with diverse suppliers and local vendors. Moreover, by fostering community partnerships, they expanded access to capital and provided valuable support to socially and economically disadvantaged businesses. Through these actions, the organization not only demonstrated a commitment to diversity but also strengthened its relationships with the community it served.

Data-driven decisions, overcoming barriers with strategic solutions, and setting realistic, sustainable goals are the cornerstones of a supplier diversity program that can lead to transformative change. As an industry professional, I emphasize the significance of continuous improvement, engaging all stakeholders, and maintaining transparency throughout the journey.

Implementing a supplier diversity program is a complex yet rewarding endeavor. By harnessing data effectively, we can make informed decisions and identify opportunities to advance diversity and inclusion. While barriers may arise, addressing them thoughtfully and proactively leads to greater buy-in and success. Lastly, setting SMART goals ensures that our initiatives remain focused, achievable, and aligned with the organization's vision. Let us forge ahead together, championing supplier diversity and leaving a lasting positive impact on the businesses, communities, and individuals we touch.

In conclusion, implementing a successful supplier diversity program requires a data-driven approach, proactive strategies to address barriers, and well-defined SMART goals. By prioritizing data management and assessment, addressing concerns through open dialogue, and setting clear objectives, organizations can create a sustainable and impactful supplier diversity program. This holistic approach fosters a culture of inclusion and equity, positively impacting both the organization and the diverse supplier community.

Action Plan

1. Data Management and Assessment: The first crucial action step is to prioritize data management and conduct a thorough assessment of your organization's current supplier diversity efforts.

2. Conduct a Focus Group: Perform a survey to identify potential barriers to success.

3. Establishing Sustainable and SMART Goals: Setting clear, measurable, achievable, relevant, and time-bound (SMART) goals is essential for the success of any supplier diversity program.

4

Designing Your Plan

In the last chapter, I laid out some potential hurdles along the way and things that you need to consider prior to implementing a system. This is very important. You need to come up with a realistic road map for your supplier diversity program, a way for the senior leadership to see that you're taking things seriously because you have a system and goal in mind. By designing your plan thoroughly, you stand a better chance of success.

Begin by taking the data you gathered in chapter two and deciphering it. Look at who the company is already buying from, whether or not any of them are already classified as diverse suppliers and so on. Once you have that information, you need to bring people into the room to discuss it. These are the senior-level project managers. The ones who are responsible for contracts. The people tied to initiatives with the government. Your job at this point is to show them the merits of the system. Get buy-in—if you don't have it already—and make sure everyone is on the same page.

Talk to your suppliers, particularly your largest ones. Ask if they have any experience in this realm and if they have any tips for your own success. They're valuable assets, and you should lean on them.

Another actionable thing to take on also deals with your vendors, and that's their contracts. Make sure you update your contracts to reflect your new stance on diversity. This way your existing suppliers know about your changes, and newer ones—particularly those who qualify as diverse suppliers—know where you stand.

The contract issue may not seem to be important on the surface, but that has not been my experience. When you don't update the contracts, employees won't take the initiative seriously—and why would they? If you're not willing to make a few tweaks to your contracts to reflect an important company value, why would they think it wasn't business as usual?

Budgets are important, obviously. Your company has a certain amount of money they can spend on purchasing, and moving to diverse suppliers could upset the apple cart, even if it's only temporary. Again, go to the data. Look at the availability of suppliers, potential problems, and so on, and this will guide your way.

Defining Success

The one thing to keep in mind when creating a supplier diversity program is to think about what success looks like. We've been in situations where clients will attempt to create supplier diversity goals based on the number or percentage of contracts awarded. While percentages and contracts awarded are a potential indicator of success, it is not always the best way to define the success of a program.

Understand that a successful supplier diversity program could mean many different things to different groups and organizations. For example, at the early stages of a supplier diversity program, success could be defined in terms of creating an effective communication strategy, implementing supplier diversity training, identifying opportunities for discretionary purchases, and/or establishing benchmarks for supplier diversity spending. Another potential outcome of a successful supplier diversity program could be mentoring or building capacity for local, small businesses.

As I've stated throughout the book, a sustainable supplier diversity program takes time, so always consider what could happen and when. Don't fall into the trap that a lot of organizations fall into by creating a plan that is only focused on increasing spending with diverse suppliers. Most of those plans fall short, because either the budget isn't there for additional funds or the interest is lost because of the cost involved.

Realigning Procurement Goals

When I think about most of the clients that we have worked with, most of their procurement departments are set up for volume purchasing. It's a competitive process that is designed for big business to generate the maximum profits for corporations and to keep the cost of doing business as low as possible. In many organizations we also see a complex vetting process that is designed to mitigate risk for the buyers. I think this is all fine and good, but at the end of the day, if the mission is to design a process that encourages participation from local, diverse suppliers, I can tell you from firsthand experience that the old way of doing business is not going to work.

My recommendation is that you take the time to explore and examine your procurement vendor process and consider areas that could be a potential barrier to success for your new suppliers. I would start with the basics, thinking about how diverse suppliers learn about opportunities in your organization. What are the criteria for doing business with your company? Does all of this make sense from the perspective of a small business?

The other thing to consider is the realignment of procurement goals to better align with supplier diversity goals. For example, if you are trying to reach more local, smaller businesses, the idea of big volume purchases might not work anymore. To be clear, I am not advocating lowering standards or even suggesting that you have to pay more to work with diverse suppliers. I am saying just the opposite. In many markets, we have found that when organizations redefined their procurement process, competition increased and pricing became more competitive.

We recently worked with a client that wanted to work with more local and diverse suppliers. They had a complex process; a lot of their larger purchases were being handled by the procurement department, but after doing a little research, they found that many of their purchasing decisions were being made at the local and regional level by mid-level managers. This organization examined what types of opportunities were being made outside of the procurement department and chose to streamline that process.

They began by creating a mandate that any purchases under $500,000 would require bids from local and diverse suppliers. They also started being more intentional about asking for information about certification as part of the purchasing process by updating their purchasing system entirely. This small shift helped this organization to change the culture of decision-makers, putting supplier diversity at top of mind. Over a period of about eighteen months, supplier diversity spending became an important KPI of how the company was doing overall, and it also spoke to the performance of managers who had key decision-making power. All of these changes made it much easier to implement supplier diversity goals on larger purchases because there was buy-in and proof of concept.

Assembling Your Team

Part of the designing process is determining accountability. This is not only who is accountable for ensuring the process goes smoothly but also each person along the chain who can and will have a hand in its success. And what does being accountable mean? What are the benchmarks and standards put in place to ensure success?

What you are doing now is putting together a team. This group of individuals will handle integrating supplier diversity into the system, have accountability for all aspects of the process, and be responsible for its success.

Obviously, making this team function well is critical. Without them humming along like a well-oiled machine, you will have issues. Look for potential problems. Are there personality conflicts? Does everyone believe in the mission? Sort out those issues early on to help ensure proper operation of the group.

Ultimately, this team's job is to purchase goods and services in the most efficient, cost-effective manner as possible. In some organizations, those people would work hand in hand with a supplier diversity professional. It's up to you whether or not that person exists in the organization, but if you want that, make sure they're built into the program.

Making Actionable Items

The goal is to take those initial conversations, plus the team building, and turn them into actionable items. There are some simple ways to do that.

Start with creating a dialogue with your local organizations. This includes your chamber of commerce, PTACs (Procurement Technical Assistance Centers), the NMSDC, Gay and Lesbian Chamber of Commerce, and the WBENC. These organizations have tons of resources to work with, and you should use them if at all possible.

PTACs in particular are great resources. You don't have to build your supplier diversity program completely from scratch. People have already done the hard work for you, and PTACs have some of that information on hand, as do the NMSDC and others.

This engagement with the community is important. As word gets out about what the company is doing, suppliers may start to appear. Diversity is an important topic in the world right now, and when businesses make moves toward improving their stance on the topic, people notice.

Your local chamber of commerce is very committed to increasing opportunities for local and diverse suppliers. It's part of their mission, so they also want you to succeed. They're helping organizations design policies and procedures, plus creating networking opportunities.

Once you've had a lot of these conversations, you may start to feel overwhelmed and like there's so much on your plate to handle. You just don't know where to start and how to get things going at your own company. Don't worry. Instead, start with the easiest thing to implement. There are a lot of ways to do this. Consider beginning with discretionary spending.

Let's go back to our construction company example from earlier in the book. They spend a lot of their money on big equipment—backhoes, cranes, etc. Those items are sent through a very structured procurement department. But discretionary purchases are the day-to-day things. It could be something as simple as what the local office needs to buy, be it cleaning or office supplies. Maybe they have a small kitchen to stock, or even have to buy new computer equipment. These are the types of things that wouldn't go through the procurement department, but instead might be purchased on a company credit card.

This is a great place to start. It is simple enough to find out where these discretionary purchases are made, and you can centralize your process around them. Once you've determined where the sales are done, you can then figure out how to integrate diverse and local suppliers into that system. Instead of going to a big chain store for printer paper, maybe they hit a smaller office supply shop in town for the same products. Every bit helps, and they are all actionable items.

The next low-hanging fruit is with expiring contracts. I've already talked about updating existing contracts, but now is also your chance to create something from whole cloth for new suppliers. You can reach out to your purchasing teams and ask what their process looks like. How do they handle bids and proposals? Have there been any discussions or dialogue with local diverse suppliers? Chances are pretty good that the answer is "No."

Now when it comes time to write these contracts, there's an opportunity to include language in the new solicitations to include some supplier diversity goals. This doesn't have to be very specific if you're not yet in a place where you can set goals.

Making Timeframes

Now that you've got all that in mind, let's talk about timeframes. First, understand that it doesn't happen overnight. This is not only an ongoing process, but one that has both short- and long-term components.

From a short-term perspective, your time frame is going to vary based on your budget, resources, and procurement timelines. All of your gathered data will play a role here as well, from bench marketing to community engagement and training.

A good thing to do in the short term is community engagement, because it can be easily implemented. Talk to local community stakeholders, unions, and other organizations that are in touch with local and diverse suppliers, as well as some of the bigger organizations mentioned previously like the NMSDC.

Now here is the thing: Some people already have really good supplier diversity programs. There is a lot to be gained by just asking for help. They may have tips and tricks that you haven't thought of yet. This also has a bonus effect, as that advice can become a part of your project rollout. You will be communicating to people both inside and outside of your company, and you need to strategize that process as well. You will definitely want to start with internal stakeholders. Consider training, which is very important. Then everyone not only knows how important it is but also how to implement things.

When you have these meetings with internal and external people, you will find some skeptics, and your job is to shift the way they are thinking about supplier diversity. Explain why it is important and dispel the different myths they have around the process. You are rewiring how they think, and that is not easy, but it can be done. Showing them the data you've discovered goes far, too.

Then there are long-term timeline objectives. Here you have lots of options, but let's talk first about building out the department. You may want to hire someone specifically to run your supplier diversity program full time. That individual would ensure the procurement team is following the procedures, and they would also adjust things as necessary.

Speaking of, you may want to plan for some long-term changes to the procurement process and the department. You are not going to get everything correct right off the bat, so making changes along the way is essential. Think of it like you are fine-tuning your system.

One thing to include in this operation is tracking data and information. This is a process, and it really needs to be thought through. You need to consider who is managing the data, where it's going, who's responsible for it, and how it is updated. I can't say it enough: it is all about the data.

As mentioned, another hurdle that you will encounter is how you're going to address the natural inclination to review supply chains through the lens of efficiency and cost-effectiveness, and explain the impact of decision-making that is dependent on outsourcing services to overseas suppliers. Again: You're not going to change that mindset overnight.

It is not necessarily your job to change that mindset, either. But what you do need to do is understand how you can add value in these different scenarios; how to shine a light on the mindset, instead of trying to change it. You can point out companies and organizations that disprove of these methodologies. If you keep adding evidence, you will eventually create a case for your argument.

But one other thing you can do to offset that way of thinking is point them to two events happening right now as I write this book that are hopefully in your past: the war in Ukraine and the COVID-19 pandemic.

The combination of these two issues has exposed significant shortcomings to the global supply chain. For example, I have an employee who is leasing a car, and it came time to turn it in to get a new lease. Thing is, the dealership is saying they don't have any cars, and it might take six months to a year until they get any. As a result, they extended our employee's lease another six months.

This is just one scenario, but you've likely experienced your own issues with that, whether it is getting a computer or a new dishwasher. The problem all comes down to the manufacturing of products and the inability to get all of the components. It is a mess.

It is also why having a diverse local supplier or two would give you a huge advantage. It translates to more sustainable outcomes for everyone and a stronger workforce. The old model isn't as effective in today's economy. It is time to move forward, and you can lead the way.

Key Performance Indicators

We've all heard the old adage that what gets measured gets done. With that in mind, I encourage our clients to create KPIs that are tied to the various aspects of a successful supplier diversity program. As we talked about earlier in the chapter, success means different things to different organizations.

Many of our clients focus KPIs on supplier diversity spending, which is the most common, but again, that does not tell the whole story.

As the demand increases for more inclusion in the corporate supply chain, we have worked with clients to develop KPIs that measure the effectiveness of the program that may include: economic impact, social impact, and diversity within diversity. We then use these as benchmarks to compare against and see how we are doing.

One of the other areas where KPIs are going to be important is within the procurement department. We encourage our clients to build in KPIs tied to employee incentives for the procurement teams. This encourages the employees to keep the supplier diversity system moving forward.

Communication Plan

Once you've developed your supplier diversity program, you are going to need a communication plan. This is an important part of the program that needs to be carefully considered and handled professionally. If you have an internal marketing or public relations team, they should be involved in the process. If you don't have an internal team, this is a great opportunity to outsource the communication plan to a local, diverse supplier.

One of the things that I often have to remind my clients about is that a communication plan is not about creating a few flyers and marketing pieces that talk about supplier diversity, it's bigger than that. It's about your company, your brand, your place in the community. It's about employee engagement, stakeholder return on investment (ROI), etc.

So what does this team do? Their goal is to communicate, both externally and internally, the changes you have made to create a diverse supplier system within your organization. This works as both PR for the company and gets other employees who didn't participate in the development of the program involved as well. It means that both outside and inside people have your back, and it also gives you more motivation to succeed. It's a win-win scenario.

My recommendation is that you think about communications early in the process, and allocate the appropriate resources in terms of time, budget, etc.

Vendor Qualifications

When creating a supplier diversity program, it is very important to clearly define and share expectations as it pertains to vendor qualifications. In my experience, I have seen some organizations that will define vendor qualifications for small businesses in the same way that they define them for larger businesses. This does not always work, and I want to be careful here not to set an expectation that standards should be lower for local, small diverse suppliers. What I am saying is that it is important to look at the standards that your organization has for doing business and make a decision as to whether or not those standards and expectations are a good fit for small companies as well as large. There isn't always a one-size-fits-all solution. Some areas you may want to consider are the following:

1. *Insurance Requirements*: Are the required limits of liability, exclusions, subrogations, and additional requirements absolutely realistic when engaging with small businesses?

2. *Financial Requirements*: We have seen situations where firms are required to produce certified financial statements. It is rare that small businesses have this unless they are an industry or government vertical that requires them to do so. The question here becomes what are you really looking to measure? What I see is that organizations want to measure capacity or determine if a company has the appropriate

resources to meet expenses for 30/60/90 days. Is this a realistic measure of a small business's capacity? Not always.

3. *Employee Size*: Some companies determine capacity by the number of employees that a firm has, and again, I ask the question, is this a true measure of a firm's ability to deliver products or services? In some markets, yes, but in others, it is irrelevant where work can be accomplished with a blend of employees and subcontractors or in situations where a vendor can potentially absorb an existing workforce (food service, security, janitorial, and other industries).

4. *Bonding*: We see small businesses locked out of opportunities all the time because they cannot get bonded. So here again, my question becomes, is there another way? We have clients who began to examine their bonding requirements and are finding alternative ways to do business while helping smaller firms to increase their capacity so they are, in fact, bonding ready.

If you have a process that is overly complicated and wrought with endless barriers, small businesses will not engage. As the demand for diverse suppliers increases, small businesses have an abundance of choices regarding who and how they do business. My recommendation is for you to think about the process you are creating and design a program that attracts the type of businesses that you want to engage with. We encourage thoughtful consideration in terms of establishing a framework that brings forward the most qualified small, diverse suppliers that meet a certain standard for doing business.

Vendor Performance

I was recently asked by a local, minority-owned business that was terminated from a project to intercede on their behalf to get an understanding of why their contract was pulled. After conducting several interviews with internal stakeholders, I heard comments like "The vendor did not deliver" or "The vendor did not perform well," but there was not a formal process in place to evaluate vendor performance, provide feedback, or improve execution through a corrective action plan. Quite frankly, this is often the norm when it comes to diverse suppliers.

You can choose to believe it or not, but I often see an unconscious bias toward small, local diverse suppliers at the very early stages of a contract. No one thinks the firms will perform well; everyone believes doing business with small firms is a risk, and therefore at the very first sign of an issue, those small firms find themselves at odds with the organization.

To eliminate those types of issues, we recommend a well-defined vendor onboarding process, and the establishment of a clear process for vendor performance and feedback.

Legal Review

Before you implement your supplier diversity program, we recommend a legal review. We have seen situations where well-intended clients have established supplier diversity programs and goals that created situations for their organizations. Some examples of that include programs that are based on race and ethnicity, or programs that potentially exclude certain groups like people with disabilities or service-disabled veterans.

We have also seen instances where the legality of a supplier diversity program has been challenged when it interrupts a certain industry or unintentionally harms another group.

I am not a lawyer, but I always advise my clients to seek legal counsel to ensure their program is fair, equitable, and meets a standard for doing business in their region. The legal review should also include reviewing all of the things we talked about in terms of process, procedure, and communication.

Action Plan

1. Write down your budget, resources, and procurement timelines. Get this data into a system like a spreadsheet so you can track it in the future, and see how you can positively move forward.
2. Create your short- and long-term timelines. You won't have all the information you need, but you can at least get ahead of the game.
3. Write up a communication strategy. You'll want one for both internal and external stakeholders, so be thorough.

For more resources on how to design your supplier diversity plan, go to https://jkasolutions.com/diversify&prosper.com

5

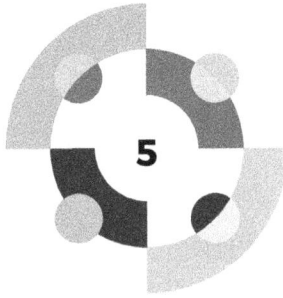

Plan Implementation

Now that you have your plan designed and a basic idea of your framework, it is time to move forward and put those plans into action. This is where things start to get more complicated, and you may run into some resistance along the way. That is OK—and totally expected.

Throughout this book, you will pick up tips on how to ensure that your supplier diversity system succeeds, but there is no single way to get it done. What you may discover are hurdles previously unknown to you or your company, or scenarios that are unique to your geographic position. I do not want to tell you this is going to be easy when it's not, but this also does not have to be like Sisyphus pushing a boulder up a hill. Come up with your framework, get your plan designed, and go to work. Remember, as long as you have followed the previous steps and have the proper buy-in from the C-suite, then you should be good to go.

One thing to remember: You will run into obstacles, and that is fine. How you react and respond to those criticisms will help determine the success of your program. Take your time to make those decisions so you can make the right choice the first time.

With that in mind, let us start implementing your plan.

Evaluating Existing Procurement Policies

In order to have a sustainable supplier diversity program, we really need to think about the people and processes that are currently established within your organization and how changing those policies may impact the system as a whole. You also have to think about the company's culture and value system.

Let me share an example to illustrate this point. Imagine a scenario similar to the movie *Wall Street*, where the company's culture revolves around greed and profit maximization. In such an environment, introducing a supplier diversity program would likely face resistance and skepticism. The company's focus on efficiency, cost savings, and volume purchasing might seem incompatible with the goals of supplier diversity. This example highlights the importance of aligning the program with the organization's values and providing compelling reasons for change.

Let's be honest: The very essence of large corporate business of corporate purchasing is all about efficiency, cost savings, and volume purchasing. There is nothing wrong with that, and for some companies, it's probably working. The question really becomes, "Is it sustainable? Is there a compelling reason to change?"

When implementing a supplier diversity program, you must be prepared to answer tough questions and address potential concerns. Having a clear understanding of your organization's procurement processes is vital. However, we've found that determining these details is not always easy, especially in large corporations with centralized procurement structures and various decision-makers. Take the time to review your organization's procurement policy to understand the ins and outs of how goods and services are procured. Some key areas to focus on include:

1. *Vendor Onboarding Process*: What is the process for becoming a vendor with your organization? Are there specific requirements that vendors must meet?
2. *Opportunity Awareness*: How do vendors learn about potential opportunities to work with your company?
3. *Purchasing Patterns:* What goods and services does your firm purchase, and when do these purchases occur?
4. *Contract Size*: What is the average size of your contracts?
5. *Responsible Parties*: Who are the key decision-makers and stakeholders in the procurement process? What are their reporting lines and performance metrics?

Once you have a comprehensive understanding of the procurement process, it's essential to engage in dialogue with the procurement team. The goal is not just to seek their buy-in but to understand their perspectives on how a supplier diversity program might impact their workflow and responsibilities. Soliciting their feedback and ideas can lead to valuable insights and help in designing a successful implementation strategy. Moreover, this could also be an opportunity to evaluate the diversity of the team itself, fostering an inclusive approach.

BUILDING DIVERSITY

A Case Study on Implementing Supplier Diversity in a Construction Company

In the competitive landscape of the construction industry, a commitment to supplier diversity has the potential to transform not only procurement processes but also the organization's overall performance. This case study explores the journey of a construction company striving to integrate supplier diversity into its procurement practices. By evaluating the existing procurement process, addressing potential barriers, and setting sustainable goals, the company aims to foster inclusivity, unlock new opportunities, and create a more resilient and successful business model.

Background

XYZ Construction Company is a reputable player in the construction industry, known for its efficiency and cost-effectiveness. While proud of its achievements, the company's leadership recognizes the lack of diversity among its suppliers and aims to rectify this. They believe that supplier diversity not only aligns with their commitment to social responsibility but also presents a strategic advantage in a rapidly evolving market.

Step One: Evaluating the Existing Procurement Process

In this first phase, the case study delves into XYZ Construction's procurement policies, procedures, and practices. The company's procurement team, together with other stakeholders involved in supplier selection, is interviewed to understand the current supplier evaluation criteria, sourcing strategies, and contract award processes. Document analysis of previous procurement decisions is conducted to identify any patterns of supplier exclusion or underrepresentation.

Findings

The evaluation reveals that the procurement process is predominantly focused on cost-effectiveness, efficiency, and experience. While these factors are crucial for successful project execution, the lack of emphasis on supplier diversity has led to a limited pool of diverse suppliers.

Step Two: Addressing Potential Barriers to Success

To gain deeper insights, the case study engages key stakeholders in candid discussions about their concerns regarding supplier diversity implementation. Interviews are conducted with procurement professionals, executives, and employees to understand their perspectives on potential challenges, including concerns about retaliation, resistance to change, and past experiences with diversity initiatives.

Findings

Several stakeholders express apprehensions about potential pushback from existing suppliers, fearing that the inclusion of diverse suppliers might compromise quality or increase costs. Additionally, concerns about the additional time and resources required to identify and evaluate diverse suppliers emerge as potential barriers.

Step Three: Setting Sustainable Goals

Armed with insights from the evaluation and barrier analysis, XYZ Construction Company proceeds to establish SMART goals for their supplier diversity program. Leadership personnel and procurement professionals collaborate to set realistic, specific, measurable, achievable, relevant, and time-bound objectives.

Goals

1. Increase the percentage of diverse suppliers in the company's procurement database by 20 percent within the first year.
2. Allocate a minimum of 10 percent of the company's total procurement budget to diverse suppliers by the end of the second year.
3. Establish a mentorship program for diverse suppliers to enhance their capacity and foster long-term partnerships.

Implementation and Outcome

With the procurement process evaluation, barrier analysis, and goal setting complete, XYZ Construction Company embarks on the Implementation phase. To ensure a smooth transition, they conduct comprehensive training sessions for the procurement team, introducing supplier diversity best practices and emphasizing the importance of inclusion and equal opportunity.

As the supplier diversity program takes root, the company engages in extensive outreach efforts, seeking out certified diverse suppliers and encouraging them to participate in bidding processes. Supplier evaluation criteria are modified to consider factors beyond cost, such as quality, innovation, and commitment to sustainability, ensuring that diverse suppliers are evaluated fairly.

Over time, the supplier diversity program proves successful, yielding tangible benefits for XYZ Construction Company. The inclusion of diverse suppliers brings fresh perspectives, innovative solutions, and enhanced community engagement. By diversifying their supplier base, the company establishes stronger relationships with local communities, creating a positive reputation and fostering long-term partnerships.

Conclusion

This case study exemplifies the transformative potential of supplier diversity in the construction industry. Through a comprehensive evaluation of the procurement process, addressing potential barriers, and setting sustainable goals, XYZ Construction Company successfully integrated supplier diversity into its core values and daily operations. As a result, the company experienced heightened innovation, enhanced community relations, and improved overall performance, positioning it as a leader in fostering diversity and inclusion within the organization.

How Does the Procurement Team Define Success?

I often encounter a common challenge among companies that hire me to focus on supplier diversity. While their intentions are commendable, they tend to become so engrossed in supplier diversity that they overlook its potential impact on other crucial departments within the organization. They often lack awareness and conscious-ness of the challenges faced by the procurement team, which can hinder progress and lead to miscommunication and resistance. It's essential to recognize that supplier diversity programs shouldn't exist in isolation; rather, they should be integrated with other departments for maximum effectiveness.

To foster successful supplier diversity implementation, we need a shift in priorities and a strong focus on collaboration between the supplier diversity, procurement, and leadership teams. It's essential for organizational leaders to take a step back and assess the potential chal-lenges that may arise when implementing supplier diversity initiatives. By being proactive and seeking a better understanding of the practices, policies, procedures, and challenges faced by the corporate purchas-ing team, leaders can ensure a smoother integration and alignment of goals.

Procurement success is often defined by getting the best goods and services on time and at the most efficient price. (I am not looking to change that, by the way.) But what if success also included expanding the pool of qualified local and diverse suppliers?

Procurement teams rarely see the connection between cost-effec-tiveness and supplier diversity. Most buyers believe if they add diverse suppliers they are going to have to spend more money, and that is a deal breaker for them. As a result, the purchases are not made and the diverse suppliers are left without options.

However, there is a major flaw in that logic, and in my experi-ence, that is just not the case. What we are seeing in the marketplace is that small, local diverse suppliers can oftentimes be more competi-tive because they don't have expensive offices, overheads, huge staffs, and stockholders to report to. In fact, one of our clients in higher education is reporting that in all instances where local and diverse suppliers were included in the procurement process, they received more competitive bids and ultimately saved their organization more money. Small local businesses also tend to buy locally, making them potentially more efficient as well.

In order to successfully implement change, business leaders must reevaluate priorities and consider the people who are involved in the process. You can't just expect things to change overnight, especially when the focus has always been getting an ROI for shareholders. They can still experience a strong ROI through an aggressive procurement process that includes qualified diverse suppliers, it is just different from what they're used to. Sometimes different is not bad. Preconceived notions tend to get in the way, however.

As the organization's priorities shift, there needs to be a clear communication strategy for procurement, influencers, stakeholders, and all those involved in making decisions about the goods and services that are purchased by the organization.

In my consulting practice, before I recommend a strategy for supplier diversity, I invest a considerable amount of time talking to various stakeholders. I find there are a lot of mixed feelings, raw emotion, and misinformation about supplier diversity. Taking the time to implement a strong discovery process is a key aspect in developing a program. Not only does it ensure the mixed feelings and raw emotion can be smoothed out, but it also helps relax all involved, making them more susceptible to change.

One of the biggest hurdles we face when implementing supplier diversity programs is getting the procurement teams onboard and fully supportive of the initiative. It's no surprise, really. The messaging around supplier diversity can be unclear, leaving our procurement professionals feeling uncertain and resistant. To create a successful supplier diversity program, we need to work closely with our organization's decision-makers in procurement and provide them with the resources and support they need to excel in their roles.

The first step is to ensure we have a crystal-clear message about the purpose and benefits of supplier diversity. Communicating the advantages of diverse suppliers, such as fostering innovation, cost savings, and community engagement, can help build support and enthusiasm.

To build trust and understanding, we must create an open and inclusive environment that encourages dialogue. Our procurement teams may have legitimate concerns about how supplier diversity could affect their existing operations, so training is a crucial aspect. All team members, whether from supplier diversity or procurement, should receive training on each other's roles and responsibilities. This cross-training not only enhances their understanding of the challenges each department faces but also encourages empathy and cooperation. By listening to their input and experiences while addressing their worries, we can foster a sense of trust and collaboration while incorporating supplier diversity into their everyday procurement activities effectively.

Continuous support is key to the success of our program. We need to provide our procurement teams with access to diverse supplier databases, offer mentorship programs to help those suppliers enhance their capabilities, and keep them updated on the progress of our supplier diversity efforts.

It's not an overnight process. We need to invest time and effort in understanding the needs and challenges of our procurement teams to develop personalized strategies that ensure their smooth transition into supplier diversity advocates. By emphasizing collaboration, communication, and unwavering support, we can overcome resistance and create an environment where supplier diversity becomes an inherent part of our procurement practices.

The leadership team plays a crucial role in facilitating this collaboration. They must take the lead in aligning the objectives of both supplier diversity and procurement, ensuring that they work hand in hand toward shared goals. By fostering a culture of teamwork and understanding, leaders can create an environment where all stakeholders feel valued and heard.

One of the resources—and we're going to talk about this in future chapters—is a champion within the organization. This is a supplier diversity team or a supplier diversity leader that they can partner with to start making the shift. Ideally, this person has some amount of power within the organization, so they can lead the charge. But even if they do not, this person should be an absolute cheerleader for supplier diversity.

To sum it up, successful supplier diversity programs require a holistic approach that transcends departmental boundaries. Companies should avoid getting lost in the singular focus on supplier diversity and instead prioritize collaboration and alignment between supplier diversity and procurement teams. Leaders should take a proactive stance, seeking to understand and address potential challenges while fostering open communication and teamwork. With a united effort and a shared vision, companies can create a supplier diversity program that delivers meaningful impact and benefits across the organization.

Adjusting Your Focus

Embracing supplier diversity is not just about meeting goals; it's a profound shift in our organizational culture. As we delve into the significance of supplier diversity, we must remember why we embarked on this journey in the first place—to create a more inclusive, equitable, and impactful business environment.

For me, supplier diversity is not a mere checkbox or a token initiative. It's about instilling a genuine commitment to diversity and inclusion at every level of our organization. We need to focus on true engagement rather than getting lost in the numbers and targets.

I've seen many organizations solely fixating on their supplier diversity goals, but that's only part of the equation. To truly transform our culture, we must go beyond meeting quotas. It requires a deep-seated cultural transformation that reshapes the way we do business, interact with others, and make decisions.

At the heart of this transformation is genuine engagement with our diverse suppliers. We can't just treat them as transactional partners. We need to build authentic, long-lasting partnerships that empower these suppliers to thrive alongside us. It's about creating a collaborative environment where everyone benefits and grows together.

For this cultural shift to take root, it must start at the top—with unwavering support from our leadership team. They need to champion diversity and inclusion, leading by example and making decisions that reflect our commitment to supplier diversity.

Engaging our entire workforce is equally crucial. Our employees need to understand the "why" behind supplier diversity and its broader impact. Through training and awareness initiatives, we can foster a shared sense of purpose and unity in our efforts.

To truly integrate supplier diversity into our culture, it can't be a standalone initiative. It must be seamlessly woven into our existing processes and decision-making frameworks. By doing so, it becomes a natural part of how we operate, and we can maximize its potential impact.

This journey may take time, and there will be challenges along the way. But we must stay true to our commitment, supporting and learning from one another. This isn't a quick fix; it's a long-term endeavor that requires consistent dedication.

Understanding the availability of qualified diverse suppliers is the backbone of a successful supplier diversity program, and it significantly impacts our relationship with the procurement department and goal setting. It's not just about setting targets and hoping for the best; it's about making informed decisions that lead to meaningful outcomes.

Let's face it; supplier diversity is a two-way street. Yes, we have the goal of creating a more inclusive and diverse supply chain, but we also need a robust pool of qualified diverse suppliers to achieve that goal. And that's where the importance of data and information comes into play.

To ensure we are connecting with the right suppliers, we need reliable and up-to-date data. As I delved into the statistics, I was genuinely shocked by the disparity between the number of certified businesses and the actual utilization of these diverse suppliers. That disconnect can hinder the progress of any supplier diversity program.

To address this issue, we must rely on reputable organizations that have a deep understanding of diversity and can provide us with accurate data. For instance, the NMSDC plays a crucial role in certifying over 11,000 diverse businesses. Additionally, the WBENC certifies approximately 7,000 women-owned businesses, and there are about 9,000 certified LGBTQ-owned businesses.

By tapping into these organizations, we gain access to a vast network of qualified diverse suppliers. Engaging with the NMSDC, WBENC, and other similar groups can be a game-changer for our supplier diversity program. They not only help us identify potential suppliers but also provide valuable resources and support to ensure the success of these partnerships. Moreover, connecting with local organizations is equally essential. Local chambers of commerce, trade associations, and business development organizations can serve as valuable allies in our quest for diverse suppliers. These groups often have a deep understanding of the local business landscape and can guide us to untapped talent and opportunities.

The key to unlocking the potential of our supplier diversity program lies in consistent engagement. It's not a one-and-done deal; it's an ongoing relationship-building process. Staying in contact with these organizations, attending events, and participating in networking opportunities will keep us at the forefront of supplier diversity and open doors to new possibilities.

However, engagement is just one part of the equation; the other crucial aspect is data management. Having access to reliable and up-to-date data empowers us to make informed decisions about our supplier diversity initiatives. We can identify trends, track progress, and assess the impact of our program accurately.

When we have the right data in hand, we can set meaningful and achievable goals. These goals go beyond mere numbers; they align with our organizational values and long-term vision. They become a part of our culture, ingrained in our decision-making processes, and supported by the procurement department.

In conclusion, understanding the availability of qualified diverse suppliers is the foundation upon which our supplier diversity program is built. By connecting with reputable organizations like the NMSDC and WBENC, we gain access to a wealth of diverse suppliers and valuable resources. Engagement and data management are pivotal in driving the success of our program and fostering a more inclusive and diverse supply chain. As we continue to embrace supplier diversity, let us remember that it's not just about meeting targets; it's about creating lasting partnerships and a thriving business ecosystem that benefits us all.

The Availability of Local Diverse Suppliers and Trust

Developing a sustainable supplier diversity program demands more than just focusing on the local channels and the current pool of diverse suppliers. While understanding the availability of qualified suppliers is crucial, we must also look beyond our immediate networks and think about ways to engage with diverse communities, build trust, and expand the pool of available diverse businesses.

Engagement is the key to unlocking the true potential of supplier diversity. Instead of compartmentalizing it as a separate initiative solely focused on MWBE participation, we should integrate it seamlessly into our overall business strategy. By doing so, we build strong, lasting connections with diverse communities, fostering an inclusive environment where everyone can thrive.

Let's consider the significance of engagement in increasing the pool of diverse suppliers. If we confine ourselves to the local channels and the current network, we may limit the number of qualified suppliers available to us. Diverse suppliers might be hesitant to come forward or may not be aware of opportunities to work with us. However, by actively reaching out and engaging with diverse communities, we create avenues for new talent to emerge.

Building trust is a cornerstone of successful supplier diversity engagement. Diverse suppliers need to know that they are valued and that their contributions matter. To achieve this, we need to go beyond lip service and demonstrate our commitment through concrete actions. This could involve collaborating with organizations that advocate for diversity and inclusion, participating in community events, or supporting initiatives that empower diverse businesses.

A crucial aspect of building trust is being transparent and honest in our intentions. When we engage with diverse communities, we should be upfront about our supplier diversity goals and how we plan to achieve them. By setting clear expectations, we show that we are serious about creating meaningful partnerships and fostering an environment of mutual respect.

Furthermore, we should consider the unique challenges and barriers that diverse suppliers may face. By being aware of these obstacles, we can tailor our engagement efforts to address their specific needs and provide the necessary support. This may include offering training, mentorship programs, or assistance in navigating the procurement process.

Expanding the pool of diverse suppliers not only benefits our organization but also contributes to a more vibrant and resilient business ecosystem. By tapping into the diverse talent and innovative ideas from different communities, we enrich our supply chain and gain a competitive edge.

This is all very important, because if you are looking to have a more sustainable supplier diversity program, you need the partnership of the local community in order to do that, which means providing them a level of access to your organization is key. When we think about access, when you think about how corporations typically do business, there often tends to be a lot of secrecy.

For example, think about the Black Lives Matter movement. After the death of George Floyd, many companies came forward and said they wanted to increase spending with diverse suppliers. They wanted to close the wealth gap, but yet when you go on their website and you look for information about how to do business with them and what they are spending, there is no information available at all. What this does is create distrust in the community. As a local diversifier myself, I see this happening all the time. It is all very reactive, as opposed to sustainable.

Corporations have to think about access and being more transparent about how they are communicating with the public. It is not enough to say "we have a new supplier diversity program." There needs to be action—*visible* action.

I saw a lot of those companies that came forward and pledged to be more inclusive in the wake of George Floyd not let the rest of us know what the actions or even results were of those projects. What I have instead seen are a lot of capacity-building programs. There is the Black Initiative with JP Morgan Chase, for example. The WBENC along with Wells Fargo and many other organizations have published all these great outreach and training programs, but there is no public information about the outcome of those programs. Often all you can find is how many people attended. But what were the results for the people who went through it? Have those individuals gained access to any more opportunities? Are there any testimonials from those folks that we're not seeing? Transparency is important here, and you need to consider the same for your own company.

A Harvard Business Review article shed light on the challenges faced by many supplier diversity programs, revealing that they have not yielded the intended results. The reality is stark, with more than 53 percent of Black business owners reporting a drastic revenue decline of at least 50 percent since the pandemic began, while the figure stands at

37 percent for white owners.[9] These disparities underscore the urgent need for real and effective action.

Transparent and open conversations are essential for understanding the root causes of these disparities and identifying opportunities for improvement. By acknowledging the barriers faced by minority-owned businesses, we can develop targeted strategies to level the playing field and foster equitable growth.

While training and education play a vital role in creating awareness and fostering understanding, the article emphasizes that tangible opportunities in the form of contracts are even more impactful. Training alone may not suffice if businesses owned by marginalized communities do not have equitable access to procurement opportunities. Procurement contracts not only provide a platform for diverse suppliers to showcase their capabilities but also solidify their position within the supply chain.

To address the existing gaps and build a more inclusive supplier diversity landscape, genuine commitment and deliberate actions are necessary to dismantle the systemic barriers that perpetuate inequalities. Moreover, apart from setting goals and targets, organizations need to devise clear strategies to measure progress and hold themselves accountable for achieving meaningful outcomes. It is vital to track the impact of supplier diversity efforts over time and course-correct as needed.

Let me share an insightful example from one of my clients who embarked on the journey of implementing a supplier diversity program. I advised them to take a cautious approach to their spending, considering past history and the availability of local and

---

9   Denise Hamilton, "Supplier diversity programs are failing black-owned businesses," Harvard Business Review, April 19, 2021, https://hbr.org/2021/04/supplier-diversity-programs-are-failing-black-owned-businesses.

diverse suppliers. The decision was rooted in prudence and thoughtful planning. However, this approach sparked mixed reactions within the community. Some expressed dissatisfaction, believing that the goals should be more ambitious, pushing for larger commitments.

While the desire for more substantial supplier diversity goals is admirable, it is crucial to strike a balance between ambition and feasibility. Taking smaller steps initially allows organizations to assess the effectiveness of their program, make necessary adjustments, and build a solid foundation for long-term success. This approach also ensures that the available pool of diverse suppliers is utilized efficiently, maximizing the program's impact.

The decision to be conservative in spending aligned with my client's commitment to sustainable growth and meaningful results. By focusing on incremental progress and measurable outcomes, they could foster an inclusive environment where diverse suppliers have a genuine chance to thrive.

Open communication with the community is essential in managing expectations and building trust. Engaging in transparent conversations and explaining the rationale behind the conservative approach can help bridge the gap between aspirations and practicality. It is crucial to convey that the commitment to supplier diversity remains firm and that the program is designed for steady expansion over time.

In this process, my role as an advocate for supplier diversity is not only to support my clients' decisions but also to foster constructive dialogue with the community. By addressing concerns and collaborating with stakeholders, we can align aspirations and build a shared vision for a sustainable and impactful supplier diversity program.

Ultimately, the journey of implementing a supplier diversity program requires navigating various perspectives and considerations.

The aim is not only to set ambitious goals but also to establish a framework that ensures success for all parties involved. By combining ambition with a prudent approach, we can create an inclusive environment that empowers local and diverse suppliers and drives meaningful change in the business landscape.

You have to be strategic, because building trust is important. All those organizations that are putting content out about their diversity efforts without context are part of the problem. These companies spend a lot of money on trying to implement their supplier diversity program, but the problem is people are not engaged. People are not bidding. People are not competing, because there is just a lack of trust.

I believe creating a program that is really focused on some of these softer skills, including patience, building trust within the community, as well as transparency, is important. If you can implement some of these skill sets into your organization and process, you will go far.

Vendor Outreach

Engagement and outreach lie at the core of a successful supplier diversity program. It is a multifaceted endeavor that requires active involvement from company leaders in sharing vital information with the identified and researched community.

Knowing and understanding the community is paramount, as it lays the groundwork for building an effective engagement strategy with specific goals in mind. Announcing the supplier diversity program to the community is a crucial step, but it's equally important to create opportunities for open dialogue and information sharing. This accessibility ensures that anyone interested can engage and learn about the opportunities within the program.

I highly encourage continuous engagement with local community organizations that possess the expertise and capacity to bolster the community. Collaborating with such organizations can not only enhance the community's potential but also increase opportunities for local and diverse suppliers.

In this engagement process, the company's leadership plays a pivotal role as they step forward to proactively communicate the organization's commitment to supplier diversity. By being transparent and accessible, they can build trust and credibility with the community, fostering a positive and inclusive relationship.

The engagement strategies may vary, ranging from community forums, workshops, and seminars to collaborative partnerships that contribute to the community's growth and empowerment. This two-way communication fosters a sense of belonging and shared purpose, aligning the company's goals with the aspirations and needs of the community. Regular interactions and updates help sustain interest and momentum, keeping the community informed and engaged throughout the supplier diversity journey.

As the program progresses, the company can leverage the insights gained from engaging with the community to tailor its supplier diversity initiatives better. This collaborative approach ensures that the program aligns with the unique needs and strengths of the community, maximizing its impact.

In our pursuit of creating a sustainable and impactful supplier diversity program, one key element that cannot be overlooked is the power of transparent outreach. Building trust, fostering collaboration, and providing clear guidance to potential vendors are all vital aspects of a successful program.

TRANSPARENT ONBOARDING PROCESS

Transparency in the vendor onboarding process is paramount to ensuring that potential suppliers have a clear understanding of the requirements for doing business with your organization. This includes aspects such as bonding, insurance, financial capacity, and business integrity. By providing detailed information upfront, you equip suppliers with the knowledge they need to meet these requirements confidently.

As part of the outreach program, consider organizing workshops or webinars to walk potential vendors through the onboarding process. These training sessions will help demystify any complexities and provide a forum for suppliers to ask questions and seek clarity. Offering this type of training or technical assistance demonstrates your commitment to supporting diverse businesses in their journey toward greater capacity and success.

PARTNERING WITH LOCAL ORGANIZATIONS

Collaborating with local organizations can be a game-changer in expanding your outreach program's reach and impact. The MBDA and the SBA are valuable partners to consider. These organizations provide resources, support services, and technical assistance to minority and small businesses, aligning perfectly with your supplier diversity goals.

By partnering with these entities, you can extend the network of support available to diverse suppliers and help them overcome challenges that may hinder their growth and participation in your supply chain. Strengthening these partnerships fosters a sense of community and emphasizes your commitment to inclusive and sustainable business practices.

ENGAGING DECISION-MAKERS
AND BUILDING TRUST

Beyond providing access to decision-makers within your organization, it's essential to be open and transparent about your current supplier relationships. Sharing information about the suppliers you are already working with reinforces the principle of fairness and equal opportunity, fostering trust within the supplier community.

Regular communication is key to building strong relationships. Ensure that your organization speaks regularly to the local community, keeping them informed about opportunities and program changes. Establishing an open dialogue and being receptive to feedback will solidify your commitment to supplier diversity and inclusive practices.

It takes time to change people's thinking; there are a lot of folks who will choose not to work with certain organizations because they do not trust them. Building trust really means having a strong community communication strategy with very clear and specific goals.

Having your employees properly trained to answer whatever questions come their way will help a lot. When your employees feel transparency and trust, your community will, too. Purchasing departments in particular, those folks who are responsible for the day-to-day operations, need to be prepared. You really have to have a good understanding of what their needs are and how the implementation of a supplier diversity program is going to impact them. As you are moving toward having a sustainable supplier diversity program, you need to ensure there is support within the organization for these individuals. I believe strongly that there should be a diversity individual or a group that is responsible for helping to take all these things into consideration and implement your program.

Vendor Engagement

Let's talk a little bit about the process of engaging with your vendors, particularly when you are moving fast. First, you need to build connections with diverse suppliers. But for a diverse supplier themselves, one of the words they hear a lot is "portal." Many corporations now will start a connection with a supplier by saying, "If you are interested in doing business with us, you have to register on our portal."

Those portals are commonly referred to by local and diverse suppliers as "black holes" because of what ends up happening: the vendors put their information in the portal, but then the loop never closes. No one ever hears back about whether or not their application has been accepted. In many cases, the registration on the portal is the first step to the corporate supply chain, not anything local.

This is equally true in a lot of government agencies. They want to make sure they have some kind of system. They are tracking the statistics around MWBE, so for them, a portal is ideal. But it can still be a black hole, and that is also frustrating to deal with on both sides of the fence.

If you are going to have people register with a portal, you want to start thinking about distinguishing your organization from the competition. To do that, you need a portal that works and is responsive.

If you're starting your own setup, you don't want to create just another portal. Because if you're looking to increase the number of diverse suppliers in your pool, folks are not going to want to continue giving people information for it to go nowhere. Many of the portals that I see out on the market regularly are not intuitive, and they are all very time consuming. The problem, ultimately, is that the average local small business does not have time to do this.

When you're thinking about creating a registration process, I would strongly recommend keeping it simple and just getting the basic information from a company. Consider having a system that does not necessarily require them to register, but instead has another intake process that is more accessible.

Pre-qualifying happens at this very early stage. What I see a lot of organizations do is they will have firms register and pre-qualify for opportunities, when in fact the small business does not even know what the opportunities are or what the pre-qualification requirements happen to be. There is an obvious disconnect there that you should make sure never happens within your own program.

My recommendation for companies and organizations looking to increase their pool of local and diverse suppliers is to create a simple process by which you can identify those suppliers on their own. With today's technology and access to the internet, there are so many ways that that can be accomplished without creating an unnecessary burden for the small business. In this way you can pre-qualify companies yourself before they come to you, or should they approach first, you can give yourself the time needed to research them.

I think it's also really important that folks have a place where they can go to get an understanding of what exactly it is that you are looking for. With most of these corporate portals, that information is buried or hidden completely. It is not clear what and when you are buying. When I talk about the process of changing mindsets, I am talking about changing the process *entirely*. There is a lot of work that needs to go into creating a new procurement system before you do your vendor outreach.

This is something you need to think about and ensure that you have the appropriate resources dedicated to building this out. After all, someone has to do this job, right? Someone would need to examine and take responsibility for posting information on a website or someplace where local small businesses and diversifiers can gain access to that information.

For example, I am thinking about some of the work I am doing with a local chamber of commerce. What they have created is something called "Power," where they are partnering with the large anchor institutions in New England. They are going to actually help those organizations increase their presence by adding information to the chamber's website.

The important takeaway here is that there are thousands of small businesses, yet only a very small number of those are certified as diverse suppliers. Companies have to be proactive and thoughtful about how they get data about local diversifiers in their area so they can make intelligent decisions. It is important for companies to share information about what they are outsourcing, but at the same time, that can be difficult without having an understanding of who is in the community.

It is a simple process to engage with local suppliers; you almost want to invite everyone, if that makes sense. With today's technology, you can easily begin to capture data while you start to work on the procurement process itself.

Process for Onboarding Diverse Suppliers

Now that you have some opportunities and a list of folks who you would like to engage with, you are ready to start onboarding.

The first thing you want to make sure of is that the process is fair. I say this because one of the things that I see in some organizations and with clients that I have been working with is only the

MWBE need to go through these portals, whereas the rest of their suppliers do not. There is an easy pathway for some suppliers, but if your organization is minority woman or veteran owned, there seems to be a separate set of rules and things that need to be done. That, in my book, is not fair.

I want to caution businesses from doing that. If we are talking about having a more inclusive process, the process by which small, local, and diverse suppliers connect to opportunities should be the same as for your larger companies. Now granted, you may want to capture information about the size of the organization as well as about their certifications. You might want to capture information about capacity, too. But my strong recommendation is to get away from having a separate process for minority women, local, and diverse suppliers, because it truly defeats the purpose.

Take your time to determine what the best method is to proceed. For example, you could start with a basic process that is simple enough for smaller companies, then work your way up from there. Then, once you have learned more about how well your process is or is not working, you can modify your onboarding process accordingly.

Again, there is no easy solution. But with a little bit of experimentation and some trial and error, you can find a method that works best for you and your specific supplier diversity system.

Identifying Barriers to Success

The other thing that is important to consider when you are looking at procurement is, again, any barriers to success. You may want to look at some of your old data; for example, if you have ever engaged with local and diverse businesses before. Were there any barriers then? And if so, how do you overcome them?

One significant challenge that diverse suppliers often face is limited access to capital. Studies have highlighted the discrimination and obstacles these businesses encounter when seeking financial resources.[10] To level the playing field and foster inclusivity, it's essential to consider how to address the capital barrier within the procurement process.

For instance, some organizations have reevaluated their payment practices by offering faster payment terms, mobilization fees, or even exploring innovative financing solutions. In this way, companies can create a more equitable environment for smaller businesses. This proactive step not only helps diverse suppliers maintain healthy cash flow but also reduces their reliance on extensive lines of credit, making it easier for them to compete in the market.

Let me share an example of a construction company that we worked with. The company was embracing this proactive approach to addressing bonding challenges. Historically, bonding requirements had been a significant obstacle for both small and diverse businesses looking to participate in large projects. The company recognized that these stringent bonding requirements were excluding many qualified suppliers and limiting competition.

To address this issue, instead of solely relying on traditional bonding measures, they considered waiving the requirement for Tier 2 subcontractors that teamed with Tier 1s. This allowed smaller and diverse suppliers with limited bonding capacity to participate in larger projects and contribute their unique expertise.

Additionally, they established mentorship and capacity-building programs to help diverse businesses strengthen their financial capabili-

---

10   Federal Reserve Bank of Atlanta, "Minority firms have harder time obtaining bank financing, fed analysis finds," January 28, 2020, https://www.atlantafed. org/economy-matters/community-and-economic-development/2020/01/28/ minority-firms-have-harder-time-obtaining-bank-financing-fed-analysis-finds.

ties. By collaborating with the local chamber of commerce and the Small Business Development Center (SBDC), they provided training, guidance, and technical assistance to suppliers, enabling them to meet bonding requirements and thrive in the competitive market.

Overall, proactive and transparent approaches such as revising payment practices, reevaluating bonding requirements, and providing capacity-building support can significantly enhance the success of a supplier diversity program. By removing financial barriers and offering opportunities for growth, organizations can create a more inclusive and collaborative ecosystem that benefits both the business and the community.

Even some of the largest companies that I'm working with now are looking for ways to be more innovative about managing barriers. It's important that the procurement team really take a look at the problem. Make sure there is a conversation and actionable decisions about what needs to change in the procurement process that will enable the organization to attract and bring on a greater variety of small, local, and diverse suppliers.

To go back to access and transparency for a moment—lack of those feelings within your community and vendors is an incredibly common barrier. This is one of the reasons why I say it's important to have the appropriate resources on the procurement team to be able to answer questions and to ensure that there is a transparent process that enables bidders to learn about opportunities.

There is a lot of information readily available about other barriers to success for small MWBE, but it's important that you have that awareness, and you need to find the balance between the processes you have for those businesses and for larger organizations, too.

Striking that balance may be difficult, but it is something that you need to manage based on your circumstances, your company, and your unique scenario. Unfortunately, there is no one-size-fits-all solution to this problem.

However, do not lose hope. Instead, as mentioned, just take your time. Again, it's more efficient to do something right the first time.

Vendor Performance Evaluations

One of the ways you can ensure the success of your supplier diversity program is to establish a protocol for giving feedback to your suppliers.

Vendor performance evaluations are a very common practice in the government space; it is a great tool that encourages a healthy dialogue between vendor and client. Some of the areas discussed often go above and beyond the goods and services that are being provided. Vendor performance evaluations explore fiscal accountability, quality control, and timeliness of performance, all key indicators that are very common with large corporations.

This opens up a lot of learning possibilities, particularly with your smaller and more diverse suppliers. You can use this opportunity to discuss any problems they may be having, for example. Say they have a cash flow problem, and your demands for product are exceeding what they are able to do, mainly because you have net-ninety day terms. That opens the door for you to help them out further by maybe adjusting your terms, or even paying them in advance, depending on the scenario.

Establishing regular check-ins with vendors can also help ensure that you have a dialogue with them before things get out of hand. It's a good way to figure out what's working and not working for you as well.

Establish regular communication protocols with your vendors and give them feedback frequently. By doing so, you will ensure a healthy ecosystem within your diverse supplier system, and you will not have any supply chain issues that are not expected.

Payment Policies

In a corporate model that is focused on cash flow management and profitability, we often see payment terms to vendors that are thirty, sixty, and ninety days in arrears. This is problematic for most small businesses, and quite frankly, with today's technology, it is an outdated business model that no longer makes sense.

When we consult with our clients, we recommend they consider more favorable terms for small businesses. Why make them wait to get paid or insist they have a line of credit? All of this costs money, which they do not want to spend. Work with your vendors to establish payment policies that make sense for both parties. We have seen lots of examples in the tech space with Google and Facebook committing to speedy cash access for diverse suppliers, ensuring they are paid within fifteen days.[11]

Today, lots of suppliers pay by check, because that has been the system of choice for decades. But now we can transfer money between accounts almost instantaneously. Anybody can take a credit card payment no matter where they are, and using apps like Venmo to transfer funds to someone is pretty simple, too.

Give your suppliers alternative payment options. If they want to be paid by wire or transfer, see what you can do to make that happen on your end. Quite frankly, I will share that for me getting paid by check is a real pain point. I cannot imagine why any large corpora-

---

11   Jennifer Moceri, "Expanding our commitments to supplier diversity," Google: Company News, March 10, 2022, https://blog.google/outreach-initiatives/diversity/supplier-diversity/.

tion is paying their vendors by check. This is definitely something to look into.

Subcontractor Reporting

Increasing supplier diversity spending can be achieved through a proactive approach that involves requiring all vendors to report on their Tiers 2 and 3 spending, or the instances when a primary contractor or vendor outsources a portion of their contract to a local or diverse supplier (Tier 2) or purchases goods from a diverse supplier (Tier 3). By implementing this requirement, you can gain better visibility into your supply chain and enhance the overall impact of your supplier diversity program.

Including clear language about supplier diversity in all contracts is a powerful way to reinforce commitment to diversity and let everyone know that it is a top priority. When vendors are contractually obligated to report their Tiers 2 and 3 spending, it creates accountability and ensures that the program's objectives are met.

Here's how implementing this approach can improve results:

1. *Enhanced Data Collection:* Requiring vendors to report their spending ensures a more comprehensive and accurate collection of data, providing valuable insights into the actual impact of the supplier diversity program throughout the supply chain.

2. *Expanded Opportunities for Diverse Suppliers:* By encouraging vendors to work with diverse suppliers for portions of their contracts, you create new business opportunities for these suppliers. This fosters the growth of local and diverse busi-

nesses and contributes to building a more inclusive supply chain.

3. *Increased Spending with Diverse Suppliers:* When vendors actively engage with diverse suppliers, it leads to a direct increase in spending with these businesses. As more vendors participate in the program, the overall supplier diversity spending grows, driving positive social and economic impacts.

4. *Improved Supplier Relations:* Including supplier diversity language in contracts demonstrates a commitment to equitable business practices. This approach can improve relationships with vendors and foster a sense of collaboration in achieving shared goals.

However, time and reporting structure should be a significant consideration with implementing this requirement. Establishing a streamlined reporting process and providing clear guidelines for data collection can help overcome these challenges. Consider implementing a centralized reporting system accessible to all vendors to streamline the reporting process, making it easier for vendors to provide the necessary information. Additionally, designating a specific team or individual responsible for managing the supplier diversity program can ensure accountability and consistency in reporting.

Of course, this is all well and good, but what if you don't have any vendors to begin with? Well, for that, you're going to need a plan. Fortunately, I've got one for you in the next chapter.

Action Plan

1. Develop a framework for examining your existing purchasing policies and procedures through the lens of inclusion. Are practices inclusive? Look at purchasing policies, process, and payments.

2. Define what an effective supplier diversity program would look like in your organization by conducting market research. Look at existing models and best practices from other similar organizations or institutions.

3. Think about how you would engage with local and diverse suppliers. First, by determining who they are and then thinking what engagement looks like. This could be something that you outsource to a local consultant.

For more resources on plan implementation, go to https://jkasolutions.com/diversify&prosper.com

6

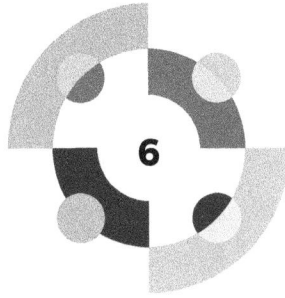

Developing a Pool
of Qualified
Diverse Suppliers

Let's face it: You cannot have a successful supplier diversity program without qualified suppliers. It is important to define what a qualified diverse supplier is early on in the process and to develop a framework where information is easily accessible to suppliers and buyers alike. I also find it necessary to continue to remind my clients about avoiding a one-size-fits-all approach to the definition of a qualified supplier. What is appropriate as a qualifier for a New York City construction firm might be completely different for a paper supplier in the Midwest. All too often I see companies creating standards for "qualified" suppliers without actually taking into account the demographics and availability of diverse suppliers, or whether or not those qualifications create any barrier to entry.

That phrase, "barrier to entry," as you've probably guessed if you've been paying attention, is key. Part of the goal of a diverse supplier program is to bring as many new companies and people into the fold as possible. The more difficult you make it for them to interact with your organization, the less businesses you will have as options for suppliers. As I have said many times, it's important to widen your lens.

In corporate DEI programs, we saw how hiring managers started looking at their practices for increasing diversity in the workplace by asking themselves if it was really necessary for a candidate to have a college degree. What they found was that, in some cases, experience in a particular field was just as valuable or even more important than a diploma from an institution of higher learning. Another example we are seeing in the current job market is the elimination of certain types of background checks or drug testing.

Do not get me wrong, I am not saying that background checks and drug testing do not have their place in determining whether a candidate is qualified or not. But what we have seen in the workplace is a shift on the approach, and when it comes to diverse suppliers, shifting our approach is at the center of what I'm talking about. Is it necessary to have an extensive background check for a supplier that will be accessing sensitive information? Of course. Is it necessary for your local food service provider? Probably not.

The point here is to think about what requirements you have to bring on new suppliers and what kinds of roadblocks you are either going to add or eliminate. What is a qualified diverse supplier to your organization, and how do we make certain that there is a balance between qualification, selection, and vendor success? This is something we will tackle in this chapter, but one you will also need to figure out with your own program.

Educating Vendors About Process

Because there is an education that needs to occur when you are rolling a program like this out, you should definitely take each aspect of the procurement process and turn it into a learning situation. For example, how does a vendor engage with your organization? What are the qualifications that vendors should have? Does that vendor need to have specific insurance? Are there other requirements that the vendor needs to address before they can even do business with you? All that information should be transparent—but also consider whether all of it is absolutely necessary.

As this program rolls out and you're working to develop a sustainable, supplier diversity program, the role of the procurement team shifts from just buying things to being more accessible to the community. Your job is to ensure that transition happens, and that it happens smoothly.

The long-term success of this program is really going to be contingent on the procurement teams having real relationships with local and diverse suppliers, providing them with consistent transparency (there's that word again!) on any aspect of the process they need to be educated on.

If you are starting with a large procurement process that is focused on global procurement, and now you are trying to have more local and diverse participation, your procurement teams have to have access to those folks. What I see a lot of corporations doing is they have a separate silo called "MWBE Firms" or "MWBE" or "Diverse Suppliers." Those folks are in one bucket versus the rest of the organization or the rest of the vendors. This needs to change. We have to start thinking of local and diversifiers as part of the overall vendor pool. We have to give those people the opportunity to interact with the procurement teams just as any other vendor would.

This goes back to the question, "What does the procurement process look like?" Because there are many organizations that I am working with where there is an extensive process for firms to pre-qualify before they can even get access to opportunities or any information. And while I think a pre-qualification process is important, it also needs to be a part of the discussion around barriers. Because if you are switching from working with large national organizations to being more purposeful about connecting with your local small businesses, there's going to be a lot of things in these pre-qualification applications that small businesses just do not have.

Consideration needs to be had and the pre-qualification or standards for doing business need to change. I am not suggesting that those standards are lowered. What I am saying is that they are evaluated to see if they align with the new goals. All of this is part of the process.

One of the ways that can be accomplished is to have supplier information sessions. Once the procurement team makes a decision about what they are going to be outsourcing and what their procurement process will look like, it is very important to have frequent supplier information sessions designed to communicate to local and diverse suppliers about the change and what is contained within it.

Recently, one of my clients came to me and said, "Hey, we want to increase our spending with Black and brown people." So I followed up with the obvious question: "What's changed?" Nothing, as it turns out. Nothing had changed within the organization, other than this new desire for more inclusivity. Point is, if you want to change one priority in your organization, then you need to think about other things that need to change as well.

The supplier information session not only needs to talk about procurement and opportunity, but it has to be a way for local, small, and diverse suppliers to engage with the organization. It goes back to some of the things I said earlier: Build trust and develop relationships over time.

A supplier diversity leader is a key component to the procurement process. That person should not be operating separately from procurement; they have to be embedded in the process. Otherwise what you end up with is two separate and distinct workflows and two separate sets of priorities. This supplier diversity leader needs to have their priorities aligned with procurement and vice versa.

Oversight by the CEO is also very important, especially before rolling a program like this out, in terms of thinking about what could go wrong and how can you get these teams to work very closely. These groups often will naturally work in opposition to each other. Procurement sees supplier diversity as a problem, an annoyance, as something they don't want to deal with. The supplier diversity leaders see procurement as the enemy. There is a big problem within an organization where that type of dynamic is going on in terms of creating a procurement process and a program that is going to succeed.

Mentorship

Mentorship is a great way to develop a pool of diverse suppliers. There are so many different approaches to mentoring, but what I have found to be the most successful is the mentor/protégé model that is frequently used on federal contracts.

Essentially, the mentor/protégé program establishes a framework where a small diverse supplier can partner with a larger company to gain access to and insights on how to successfully deliver products and services to a government agency.

The goal of the program is to assist the protégé with developing the necessary skills that will enable them to increase their capacity—something we'll talk more about in just a moment. Support may include things like:

1. *Access to back-office services* such as inventory management, manufacturing, marketing, and strategic planning.
2. *Financial assistance* in the form of equity investments, loans, and bonding.
3. *Procurement assistance*, including helping firms navigate through the complexities of identifying opportunities and completing the necessary forms, documents, and pre-qualifications.
4. *Business development strategies* and human resource management strategies for hiring, retaining, and training the best talent.

The mentor/protégé relationship is a formal program that is administered through the SBA or the buyer. The agreement defines the role of the mentor and the protégé, and establishes specific timelines for service delivery and milestones that the parties agree to.

There are two roles here that you can play. The first is when you are getting your diverse supplier program going. If you can find a mentor, then you can be their protégé and learn the ropes as you go. This is a great way to get the knowledge you wouldn't have otherwise, and pick up all the benefits listed above.

But once you get your program a little bit more steady, now the roles can reverse. You can mentor another company and get them going strong. Or, should the opportunity present itself, you could mentor one of your diverse suppliers and move them and their business along, too.

All of these relationships work very much to your benefit. There are some stigmas associated with being a protégé, but believe me, they are all made up. Get through whatever preconceived notions you may have about the role and dive in. The benefits are amazing.

We have seen some of our clients in the private sector adopt this type of a model, and it works. Mentoring is a powerful tool that goes a long way toward developing a qualified pool of suppliers.

Discretionary Purchasing

My experience with discretionary purchasing programs is largely from my work with New York City. The way discretionary spending typically works, the buyer will set aside a certain portion of their procurements within a specific financial threshold that will be earmarked for diverse suppliers. The city of New York started out by creating opportunities ranging from $1 up to $20,000 for professional services, and $35,000 for construction. This program made it easier for smaller local businesses to gain access to opportunities and learn about the nuances of doing business with the government. The city also established a small purchase program that started out with procurement of $100,000, which eventually led to the MWBE Non-Competitive Program that increased the value of procurements to diverse suppliers up to $1 million. This program continues to be successful in New York City as a capacity builder, enabling MWBEs to access government contracts that were previously out of reach for them and as a result fostering a more inclusive procurement process contributing to the growth and development of small businesses within the community.

Let's explore some of the key advantages of discretionary purchasing programs:

1. *Faster Procurement Process:* Since a predetermined percentage of contracts is set aside for diverse businesses, the procurement team can efficiently identify eligible suppliers and expedite the contract award process. This reduction in the procurement timeline benefits both the organization and the suppliers, as it allows projects to move forward more swiftly.

2. *Increased Supplier Diversity Spending:* By reserving specific opportunities for diverse suppliers, corporations can ensure that a fair share of contracts goes to underrepresented businesses. This commitment to supplier diversity enhances the organization's reputation and demonstrates a strong commitment to inclusivity and social responsibility.

3. *Simplified Reporting and Compliance:* Incorporating supplier diversity language in contracts allows organizations to track and monitor supplier diversity spending more effectively. This reporting process reduces the administrative burden on the procurement team and ensures transparency and accountability in supplier diversity initiatives.

4. *Enhanced Community Impact:* By awarding contracts to local and diverse suppliers, organizations contribute to job creation and economic growth within the community. This community engagement fosters positive relationships with stakeholders and strengthens the organization's bond with the regions they serve.

5. *Increased Innovation and Competitiveness:* By engaging with a diverse supplier base, organizations can tap into new and

diverse skill sets, leading to increased innovation and competitiveness. Diverse suppliers often offer specialized products and services, providing the organization with a competitive edge in the market.

6. *Improved CSR Profile:* Discretionary purchasing programs align with an organization's CSR initiatives, enhancing their reputation as a socially responsible company. Supplier diversity demonstrates a commitment to equitable business practices, diversity, and inclusion, which resonates positively with customers, investors, and the community at large.

7. *Reduced Time and Paperwork:* When an organization implements discretionary purchasing programs, it streamlines the procurement process by reserving specific opportunities for diverse suppliers. As a result, the time and paperwork required to award contracts are reduced. Pre-established contract frameworks and simplified evaluation criteria enable quicker decision-making, benefiting both the organization and the suppliers.

You may not have those same opportunities with your city or state. But there are other similar programs out there, such as the federal Simplified Acquisition Program, which, like NYC's discretionary purchasing program, earmarks opportunities for small, diverse suppliers. The key element of these programs is that the process of acquiring a contract should be more straightforward, less time consuming, and easier all the way around. Keep an eye out for these types of programs, as they should work to your benefit.

I have a handful of clients using a similar procurement methodology in the private sector, wherein the concept of discretionary purchasing can be tailored to fit the organization's unique requirements and resources. By setting aside a dedicated spending threshold for diverse suppliers, private corporations can actively contribute to building an inclusive supply chain while encouraging the growth of MWBE and significantly reducing the time and paperwork involved in awarding contracts. Through this approach, the private sector can not only enhance supplier diversity but also streamline their procurement processes.

In large organizations, micro purchases occur all the time outside of the procurement department. You'd probably be surprised to see how much is being purchased under the $100,000 threshold every single day. Everything from pens and paper to office decorations can count toward the overall number, so start digging into your purchasing and see what kinds of options that you have as well.

I love this approach and can say that it definitely does build capacity; however, it does require thoughtful planning and attention to detail. I have seen situations where the procurement process is simplified, but everything else about doing business as the entity is difficult for the supplier. An example of this would be the process for submitting an approved invoice or getting paid. Sometimes there are long, drawn-out paperwork processes just to get money to your supplier, and that is no fun for anyone.

By streamlining payment processes and paperwork, and providing clear and accessible guidelines for diverse suppliers, companies can foster a collaborative and rewarding relationship. Investing in efficient supplier onboarding, transparent communication, and prompt payment practices demonstrates a genuine commitment to supplier diversity and creates a positive impact on the supplier's ability to thrive within the business network.

Ultimately, the success of the discretionary purchasing approach lies in the harmonious alignment of procurement efficiency and supplier-friendly practices. By being attentive to the supplier's journey and alleviating unnecessary burdens, companies can foster a mutually beneficial relationship that empowers diverse suppliers to flourish and contribute to the organization's growth and success.

Capacity-Building Programs

Another problem that we are experiencing in some markets is a capacity issue. For example, I have less than fifty employees and there is only so much we can give. This means your diverse supplier program needs to have realistic expectations for each of your vendors, as well as the capacity to take on more if need be.

It is important to think about capacity building. Small businesses operate differently from how larger firms operate, and this is a skill set that small businesses are going to need to develop in order to have long-term success with a large corporation or a government agency.

Capacity building, in essence, is about making sure a business can grow and scale to handle the capacity that you need them to produce. If you are the person buying their products, then you are helping them—through your purchases—to expand. But they may not automatically convert that information into what they need to expand their capacity.

Now this isn't as much of an issue with a large corporation, because they either have the capacity to produce what you need or a plan to get there. Small businesses, however, may not have that structure in place. If it is in your best interest for them to flourish, then you should offer assistance wherever you can—especially when it comes to enhancing communication, navigating procurement processes and finances, networking, and fostering cultures of innovation and continuous improvement.

Investing in capacity-building strategies can significantly support supplier diversity goals in several ways:

1. *Increased Competitiveness:* Capacity building equips diverse suppliers with the necessary skills, knowledge, and resources to compete on a level playing field with larger, more established suppliers. This enhanced competitiveness allows them to win contracts and contribute to the organization's supplier diversity goals.

2. *Expanded Supplier Pool:* By investing in capacity building, organizations can help nurture and develop a more extensive pool of qualified diverse suppliers. This expansion increases the diversity of available suppliers, providing more opportunities for supplier diversity spend.

3. *Long-Term Relationships:* Capacity-building initiatives often involve mentorship and coaching programs, fostering long-term relationships between large organizations and diverse suppliers. These relationships can lead to sustained partnerships, encouraging repeat business and ongoing support for diverse businesses.

4 *Reduced Barriers:* Many diverse suppliers face barriers, such as limited access to capital, technology, and business networks. Capacity-building efforts can address these barriers, creating a more inclusive and supportive environment for diverse suppliers to thrive.

5. *Innovation and Creativity:* Diverse suppliers often bring unique perspectives and innovative solutions to the table. By investing in capacity building, organizations tap into this diversity of thought, fostering a more creative and dynamic supply chain.

6. *Mitigated Risks:* Well-equipped suppliers are more likely to deliver high-quality products and services consistently. Capacity building can help mitigate risks associated with supplier performance and ensure a reliable supply chain.

7. *Aligned Business Goals:* Capacity-building initiatives can be tailored to align with an organization's specific supplier diversity goals. By investing strategically in supplier development, organizations can better achieve their diversity objectives.

8. *Enhanced Reputation:* Organizations that actively invest in capacity building and supplier development demonstrate their commitment to supplier diversity and inclusion. This proactive approach can enhance their reputation among customers, employees, and stakeholders.

9. *Sustainable Impact:* Capacity building creates lasting impact and empowerment within diverse supplier communities. As diverse suppliers grow and succeed, they contribute to economic growth and job creation in underserved communities.

In terms of capacity building, I do not think we need any more classes. In fact, that is the one thing that you don't want to do. There are so many organizations out there already doing this work. The NMSDC and the MWBE, and Goldman Sachs, for example, have really effective capacity-building programs in place. If you determine that training is an issue for your vendor pool, my suggestion would be to partner with local organizations who already have well-established programs, because we do not need another one.

What we do need to see is more transparency on the procurement process. Before we fill out paperwork or do anything extra, let's define what the opportunities are. Look at the size and scope of the project so that small businesses can make intelligent decisions about whether or not it makes sense for them to go through this exercise.

One of the things that I am seeing that is working really well is creating levels of opportunity where smaller firms can gain access to opportunities and learn how to do business with your organization. They will then grow with the process.

Take a look at your own program and start taking the perspective of the supplier. Walk through your process as if you were a potential new supplier and see what obstacles are in your way, then work hard to minimize them.

New York City's discretionary purchasing program, for example, has helped eliminate barriers by making opportunities available to local MWBE. I have seen the companies that participate in these opportunities learn and then take their newfound knowledge to grow. In other words, they're getting the skills that they need on the job and getting the support they need.

That means there is a minimal risk to bring on a firm that can perform at a lower level. Instead of having firms continue to go through all of these different training programs that they did before—which, quite frankly, I rarely saw increased capacity—what they ended up doing is going from one program to another. So this is something that requires a little bit of thought.

If you are the company looking for a supplier, would you rather write twenty checks or just one? That is capacity building—helping to get a company to that next level where they can handle larger projects—but this requires a little bit more thought in terms of what is the best way to build capacity, and it is not by putting on another class.

Another way that we see firms building capacity is through subcontractor relationships. This is a best practice that the Billion Dollar Roundtable has that basically says when they award a contract to a minority or a woman-owned business, that business also needs to spend at least 15 percent of their contract with other local MWBE, effectively nurturing a network of supportive suppliers.

By fostering subcontractor relationships, the benefits ripple throughout the local business ecosystem. The practice not only enhances the capacity of the primary contractor but also empowers smaller businesses by providing them with more significant opportunities to grow and contribute to the supply chain.

Through networking and tiered relationships, small businesses can strengthen their competitive edge, develop specialized skills, and access new markets. Ultimately, this collaborative approach to capacity building empowers diverse businesses to achieve lasting success and contribute significantly to the broader economic landscape.

Capacity building can be multifaceted. There could be a learn-as-you-go environment that you are making available to businesses that have the capacity to grow with your organization. So if they are successful at $100,000, maybe there is an opportunity to continue adding to them.

Quite frankly, that is how I built my business. It all began with a modest $30,000 contract, which provided a valuable learning opportunity to navigate the intricacies of doing business with an agency. This experience allowed me to gain a deeper understanding of the nuances that procurement departments entail. From labor management to law compliance, invoicing follow-up, and a plethora of other elements, successful engagement with a procurement department requires a comprehensive approach. And the more a supplier and an organization collaborate through this process, the more incremental growth both will see.

Today, our company has grown into a thriving seven-figure enterprise. This achievement didn't come from attending more classes or workshops, but rather from gaining access to real opportunities that allowed us to learn and grow. It is crucial to extend a similar platform to your suppliers as well.

Empowering your suppliers with practical opportunities to engage and contribute to your organization's success can be transformative. Instead of relying solely on traditional training programs, offering them actual projects and contracts will enable them to learn on-the-job, apply their skills, and adapt to the intricacies of doing business with you. Together, you can forge a mutually beneficial path toward success.

Tracking Procurement Spending

When it comes to tracking procurement spending, simplicity is the key to success. Many companies tend to overcomplicate the process, delving into complex spreadsheets and intricate tracking systems for diverse spending. Unfortunately, this approach often leads to confusion and unnecessary friction.

The best course of action is to keep it straightforward. Avoid unnecessary complexities that could deter people from actively engaging with your supplier diversity program. Instead, opt for user-friendly tracking methods that streamline the process and encourage widespread participation.

By reducing friction and simplifying the tracking process, you make it easier for everyone involved to stay committed to supplier diversity goals. Embrace a straightforward approach that aligns with your organization's culture and goals, allowing you to effortlessly monitor and celebrate your progress toward a more diverse and inclusive supplier base. Remember, simplicity paves the way for success in supplier diversity tracking.

My suggestion is to start with what you already have. There is a way to enhance your current system, you just need to determine how to do it. You want to avoid—at all costs—creating a separate system, because it is more work for everyone. When you do that, I have found the procurement and accounting departments resist. It is another thing to cast a negative light on the supplier diversity program, because it is just one extra job that everyone has to do in order to make it work.

The tricky part here is that every company has a different system to work with. Fortunately, those systems are usually customizable in one way or another. Again, you want to lessen the friction involved, so do not try to reinvent the wheel.

Let's try instead to keep this as simple as possible, and maybe create a program that tracks the spending for all of your vendors. It could be a simple enhancement made to your current system, adding a certification, or putting in a space for a provision that you can track Tier 1 and Tier 2 spending as opposed to creating a new system from whole cloth. It's just much easier to do.

I would also talk to vendors. It is surprising what you will discover when you are working with some of the larger group purchasing organizations. They already have things in place that you may be able to learn from. By talking to vendors first, you find out what you need to do before you find yourself making changes to an entire program. And you are doing those changes with the knowledge of what would impact the vendors as well as getting their feedback. What you are doing is increasing the bond in your partnership, which will bring the two of you closer in the long term.

Another important point is to collaborate with your internal teams. Let's go back to the concept of the marriage between supplier diversity and procurement. Find out the key data points that the supplier diversity teams are going to measure every single month. Again, simplicity is key, because if you overcomplicate this, the whole thing turns into a nightmare. Ensure that before you make any changes to your process, that you are bringing in all of the stakeholders into the room.

Consider things like where these individuals are registering. What kind of database are they using? Does it work with QuickBooks and other accounting software out there? You have to take these things into consideration so that it is not this multilayered program. Instead, find a way that these systems can talk to each other. That way if a person is registering, you have data about procurement spending, invoicing, and whatever other information you need to track.

Recently I've had the opportunity to work with a number of subject matter experts that have really helped to define what this process looks like. I strongly suggest going that route instead of struggling with implementing something on your own. Consider bringing on a consultant that really understands supplier diversity dashboards. Someone who knows the key metrics that need to be tracked for your industry, and the various systems that are currently being utilized within your organization. For example, what do you need to track regarding procurement spending? A consultant can be really helpful.

Your accounting department is only going to be familiar with the accounting software they use, and might become more of a hinderance than you expect in the process. By working with a subject matter expert who has a 360-degree view of both accounting and procurement, you will see that they have an understanding of all the different systems within your organization and use that information before they suggest any changes.

Here is something that I discovered recently within my own business. We, like many companies, use a variety of different pieces of software. We use Salesforce as our CRM, for example, and we recently started using HubSpot on top of that. The more software platforms that I brought in, the more I realized the complexities around managing all of this data.

That is when I learned about APIs. API stands for Application Programming Interface, and they are a way that data from multiple applications can talk to each other. That way you do not have to change how you are doing business. How did I learn about APIs? I discovered all of it through working with a subject matter expert.

Another important thing to do is learn from and get best practices from professional organizations. There are a lot of different ones depending on what industry you are in, but I always like to start with the NMSDC, the WBENC, and those organizations that are tracking and working with companies at the Billion Dollar Roundtable.

These groups publish a lot of data and information about how companies are handling their own supplier diversity programs right now. Definitely look to them for their expertise, as it will be a good marker moving forward.

And again, it's important to have an effective vendor onboarding strategy. Oftentimes, we will take on a client and almost every single time we discover that they are already working with local and diverse suppliers but they did not know it. They did not have a system to track information—something that would have been gathered during a vendor onboarding process. One of the things we've done with our current client base to change up their onboarding process is to include multiple data points so we are able to capture information about local and diverse suppliers. Also, as part of this onboarding strategy, we have vendors include their Tier 1 or Tier 2 spending as part of the information they share with us.

By tracking procurement spending you can increase the effectiveness of your supplier diversity program by getting your vendors to track how much they are spending with diverse suppliers as well—and almost requiring them to do so, too.

Action Plan

1. Survey your current suppliers to make sure you have a really good understanding of any potential issues within your organization that could impact the success of your supplier diversity program. In the course of doing that, consider talking to local and diverse businesses who you might want to work with in the future.
2. Identify partners in the community that support your mission. There's no shortage of organizations and programs out there who can help your supplier diversity program succeed.
3. Look at your technology stack and see if there are any changes necessary to help your supplier diversity program. Do you need to work with someone to help your software work with each other?

For more on how to implement a successful supplier diversity program, go to
https://jkasolutions.com/diversify&prosper.com

7

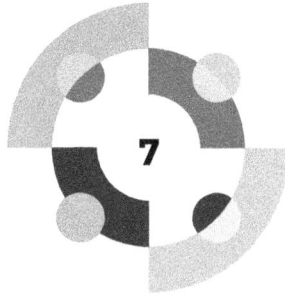

What You Need to Know Now

There is this saying that you have probably heard before: "You don't know what you don't know." It is a phrase I have heard before, and also something I run into regularly. It is about the unforeseen problems that come up when you start anything new, whether it is a supplier diversity program or a remodel on your home.

This section of the book is dedicated to shedding light on those unforeseen obstacles that have the potential to significantly impact the success of your program. By bringing them to your attention now, my aim is to empower you with valuable insights, enabling you to find innovative solutions and enhance your overall system.

I understand that this journey may be frustrating at times, and that's completely natural. Building and refining a supplier diversity program is a process that requires persistence and determination. However, I firmly believe that there is a clear path forward, waiting for you to conquer those obstacles with unwavering resolve.

Vendor Pre-Qualification

As we talked about in the last chapter, vendor pre-qualification can be complicated, so let's get into some more specifics.

The supplier faces the daunting task of filling out multiple applications, potentially involving certification applications, for each organization. This process alone entails a significant amount of paperwork and does not guarantee them access to the desired opportunities. In fact, they may not even know what opportunities are available until they are eventually approved.

This situation raises a critical issue—barriers to entry. Suppliers invest considerable time and effort, providing sensitive data such as personal and business tax returns, without any assurance of fruitful outcomes. The lack of transparency and feedback during the qualification process further compounds frustration and uncertainty.

As you develop your own supplier qualification system, it's crucial to prioritize simplicity. Streamlining the process can significantly reduce burden and increase supplier willingness to engage with your organization. Consider limiting the number of certifications required, or better yet, explore whether certifications are necessary at all for certain opportunities.

By implementing a more transparent, efficient, and respectful qualification process, you can break down barriers and foster a more inclusive supplier diversity program that attracts a diverse range of qualified suppliers, enriching the pool of opportunities and driving meaningful impact.

THE CERTIFICATION PROCESS

As an MWBE seeking to become a supplier for a government agency, you might find yourself grappling with the need to complete multiple separate applications for each certification.

For instance, if you are a service-disabled, small business owner veteran, the number of applications multiplies to six—each requiring a substantial amount of information. This disparity places an additional burden on diverse suppliers, creating extra hurdles that non-diverse suppliers do not have to face.

You might think that an ideal solution would be the establishment of a universal certification recognized across all government agencies, large corporations, and organizations in between. Streamlining the certification process would level the playing field, providing all businesses, regardless of their diversity status, with equal access to opportunities. But this doesn't exist—yet. Which is why it's all the more essential to be transparent in your contracting process while utilizing all training resources available to you.

Access to Capital

As I mentioned briefly earlier, one of the larger problems facing MWBE today is access to capital. To state the obvious, companies need money to function. Sometimes, when starting up a business, the amount you have on hand is low, so you go looking for investors or ask a bank for a loan. The resulting capital propels your business forward, you become a success, and every time you walk down Main Street confetti rains from the air.

Now initially, you might think the issue is that it is difficult for MWBE to get capital, but I want to challenge that concept a little bit.

I don't think the problem is really how access to capital is discussed, particularly to MWBE. The problem, as I see it, is the education surrounding access to capital, and how that affects diverse suppliers. There is also a lack of attention given to the details of the process, which makes it seem complex and difficult to navigate. After all, there are different types of capital and different standards for accessing said capital, and those are things that not everyone understands.

Instead, what should happen is education. Larger organizations and groups should help educate MWBE owners about everything related to the topic. This includes you, should you have a supplier who needs assistance. Alternatively, if there were resources available to these suppliers, or an available mentor, that would also be good.

Why you? Take a moment and step back. I have already discussed how some small businesses come into being. An ex-convict starts their bakery because nobody else will hire them, or a mother of four starts making T-shirts with tools purchased at her local craft store and selling them online. They do not necessarily have an MBA or even any experience running a business. So why would they know how to get more money to grow their enterprise?

If part of the logic for why you started the diverse supplier plan at your organization is to help local people who have MWBE, then giving them some extra guidance should not be a big stretch. By giving them the tips that you learned either in school or by going through life, you may play a role in taking their business up another level. That, in turn, helps you and your business by giving you a stable partner for your purchasing.

This also extends to them and their own purchasing plans. If they pay their suppliers on time and review their own procurement processes, that will help everyone down the chain. Timely payments can be a game-changer for subcontractors. When they receive their payments promptly, it helps them manage their cash flow better, which is crucial for their day-to-day operations. It gives them the stability to focus on delivering top-notch products and services, and it empowers them to invest in their growth and capacity.

If I have a good relationship with my business partners, my clients are paying me on time, and I am making a good margin, then there is no reason for me to go to a bank for a loan. But if not, or if I need help, that education and partnership from you or your company can take me far. Especially if payment windows go from ninety to sixty to even thirty days, or if there is a supply chain finance program in place, which would allow suppliers to be paid early from a financial institution at a discount.

Thinking of it a different way, if you are going to ask your suppliers to complete all these applications and get all of these certifications, you could provide an additional benefit: access to a partnership, and easier and quicker access to capital. It's a win-win situation.

Economic Impact

Defining the success of supplier diversity programs through the lens of economic impact is crucial to understanding their true value and effectiveness. By evaluating supplier diversity programs in this way, organizations can gain insights into various areas of significance, such as:

1. *Job Creation:* Supplier diversity programs often lead to increased opportunities for diverse businesses, resulting in job creation within these communities. According to the NMSDC, diverse businesses create and sustain more than

1.8 million jobs, and $136.4 billion in total wages earned, across the United States.[12]

2. *Revenue Generation:* Diverse suppliers contribute significantly to the economy through revenue generation. The NMSDC reports that minority-owned businesses contribute $482.1 billion in total economic activity driven through certified MBEs.[13]

3. *Community Development:* Supplier diversity programs can have a profound impact on local communities, especially those historically marginalized. Supporting diverse suppliers allows them to invest in their communities, leading to improved infrastructure, educational opportunities, and social services.

4. *Innovation and Creativity:* Diverse suppliers often bring unique perspectives, innovative ideas, and creative solutions to the table. Embracing diversity in the supply chain can lead to enhanced problem-solving and product/service development.

5. *Economic Resilience:* Diverse supply chains offer greater resilience during economic downturns or crises. By having a wide range of suppliers, organizations can adapt more effectively to disruptions in the market.

6. *Increased Market Share:* Research from the Hackett Group shows that companies with strong supplier diversity programs

---

12   "NMSDC Releases Its Yearly Minority Businesses Economic Impact Report," National Minority Supplier Development Council, June 11, 2023, https://nmsdc.org/news/nmsdc-releases-its-yearly-minority-businesses-economic-impact-report/.

13   Ibid.

achieve, on average, 133 percent greater return on procurement investments than their peers.[14]

7. *Enhanced Corporate Reputation:* Organizations committed to supplier diversity are often viewed more favorably by customers, employees, and investors. Demonstrating a dedication to economic inclusion and social responsibility can enhance a company's overall reputation.

8. *Global Competitiveness:* Embracing supplier diversity fosters a competitive advantage for businesses, as diverse suppliers often bring diverse perspectives and knowledge of international markets, supporting global expansion strategies.

Let me share a compelling real-life example that illustrates the economic impact of supplier diversity in the context of the COVID-19 pandemic. One of my clients had implemented a supplier diversity program approximately a year before the peak of the pandemic, and they had started laying the groundwork for a more inclusive supply chain. Little did they know that this program would prove to be a game-changer during the crisis.

When the pandemic struck, it disrupted global supply chains, causing major delays and shortages for many large national suppliers. This presented a significant challenge for my client, who relied heavily on these national suppliers for their goods and services. However, amidst the chaos, they discovered an unexpected solution—local diverse suppliers. These businesses, often operating on a smaller scale and closer to the community, were more agile and better equipped

---

14   The Hackett Group, "Top supplier diversity programs broaden value proposition to drive increased market share, other revenue opportunities," February 16, 2017, https://www.thehackettgroup.com/top-supplier-diversity-programs-broaden-value-proposition/.

to adapt to the rapidly changing circumstances. They could quickly pivot their operations to meet the urgent demands of the pandemic.

As a result, my client's reliance on local diverse suppliers proved invaluable during those critical times. These suppliers provided the necessary goods and services when their larger national counterparts faced delays and shortages. The economic impact was twofold: not only did my client have access to essential supplies, but they also supported the local economy by investing in and sustaining diverse businesses.

This example showcases the economic resilience and adaptability that supplier diversity programs can offer in times of crisis. By fostering relationships with local diverse suppliers, organizations can create a more flexible and robust supply chain. Furthermore, this scenario illustrates how supplier diversity programs contribute to local economic growth. The revenue generated by these diverse suppliers circulates within the local economy, supporting jobs, infrastructure, and social development.

Embracing diversity in the supply chain not only enhances a company's ability to navigate crises but also strengthens the economic fabric of the community. It showcases how investing in diverse suppliers is not just about meeting diversity goals but about creating a more resilient, adaptive, and economically impactful business ecosystem.

Resistance

When I first started doing this work, I wanted to change the world. I thought since there had been no significant changes in the supplier diversity industry for the past forty years, that somehow I would show up at a client's door full of ideas, ready to get to work, and change would happen. What is really interesting is that I could have never imagined the amount of resistance I would get from my own clients when trying to make a shift. This was a true blind spot for me.

Now, having successfully implemented a number of successful supplier diversity programs, I think it is important for leaders to anticipate resistance and plan for it. I say this because change is difficult, especially in large corporations. People get comfortable with the way they have been doing things; I find that no one really likes to change—this is especially true of large corporations.

But before I dive into my thoughts about change management, I also wanted to share some of the ways that resistance shows up, and the potential impact it has on folks like me, the implementers of supplier diversity programs.

One of the key ways that I see resistance show up when talking about supplier diversity is in the numbers. There will always be someone on the team who will ask the question as to whether the organization is willing to pay more to collaborate with diverse suppliers. The truth is no one wants to pay more, and the answer to the question is always "no"—but that is the wrong question.

This resistance is arguably the number one thing I hear, and there is a certain logic to it. As I have already mentioned (and you probably know from your own experiences) national suppliers have the economies of scale working in their favor. The logical inclination is to go with them because that scale will bring you lower prices. However, we have found time and time again that when the competition pool includes local, qualified, diverse suppliers, it almost always results in savings for the corporation.

Another key way I see organizations resist the inclusion of diverse suppliers is by standing by their overly complicated vendor application process. To be clear, I have never met a qualified diverse supplier that has received a contract when participating in that kind of process. So many corporations stand behind these types of vendor qualifications, certifications, and onboarding processes even though they are inefficient, expensive, and time consuming—all in the name of making sure that diverse suppliers are "qualified." Resistance.

If you want to establish your own supplier diversity program, those people who continue to reinforce those processes are part of your resistance, and you must address their concerns head-on. They will speak of those certification programs and the vendor qualifications as if they are required, when that is very much not the case. Think about your approach to solving this resistance before you get your program started and you will be ahead of the game. Ask yourself if the current processes truly serve the intended purpose of identifying qualified suppliers or if they inadvertently hinder the inclusion of diverse businesses. Consider alternative methods to assess suppliers' capabilities and qualifications that are more inclusive and accessible to diverse suppliers.

Finally, one of the worst forms of resistance is to bring a supplier diversity professional into your organization and then not empower them. I see this happen in so many groups where the supplier diversity professional is in a silo all by themselves. In those scenarios, their job is to engage with diverse suppliers and bring awareness to the program with very little or no decision-making authority. Quite frankly, this practice not only undermines the entire supplier diversity community, but it is detrimental to the supplier diversity professional, often resulting in depression, anxiety, and health issues. It is a job that goes nowhere, and when times are tough, they are the first to be let go.

This could be your exact scenario too, particularly if you are the one pushing for the program. How do you fight this? It depends on your organization. If you have any power, make sure that your role— or the role of the supplier diversity professional—is not shoved away.

Keep them close and integrate that role deeply into the procurement process and protect them. They (and/or you) are the best hope to keep the program alive.

Let's take a moment and put this into context with an experience I had with a global organization. My team was called in to help ensure that a certain percentage of contracts were awarded to local diverse suppliers. I was asked to review solicitation responses and then sit in on pre-award presentations. However, my enthusiasm soon waned as I realized that I had limited decision-making authority and was isolated from crucial processes.

Despite having the title and responsibility of managing the supplier diversity program, I found myself operating in a silo. My input was often disregarded, and critical decisions were made without considering the impact on supplier diversity goals.

I was excluded from high-level meetings where strategic decisions were made, leaving me uninformed about the organization's sourcing strategies and upcoming projects. Consequently, I could not proactively identify opportunities to engage diverse suppliers or advocate for their inclusion in relevant contracts. This lack of empowerment not only affected the success of the program but also took a toll on my own morale and well-being.

The consequences of this disempowerment were significant. The supplier diversity program struggled to gain traction, and the organization missed out on the numerous benefits that a robust supplier diversity initiative could have brought. Furthermore, my passion for advancing supplier diversity was dampened, and I felt demotivated and disheartened in my role.

A successful supplier diversity program requires genuine commitment and support from leadership, fostering an inclusive culture where supplier diversity is truly valued.

In my case, had I been empowered to collaborate with other departments, participate in strategic planning, and influence key decisions, the supplier diversity program could have flourished.

Do not let anyone go through this on your watch. If you are the one to establish or manage your supplier diversity program, make sure this never happens to a potential vendor of your own. That is not the kind of resistance we need.

Empowering supplier diversity professionals is a critical step in dismantling resistance to supplier diversity initiatives. By valuing their expertise and empowering them to make a real impact, organizations can build a more inclusive, resilient, and successful supplier diversity program that benefits everyone involved.

It Takes Time

You may be asking yourself, "If things are that bad with my supplier diversity clients, why not just quit?" Trust me, I have thought about it many times, and in some cases, ones where I felt that there was not a true commitment, I left. However, in other situations I had to draw on my experience as a supplier diversity expert, knowing that creating a sustainable supplier diversity program takes time.

This is one of the most important messages that I want to communicate to you: It takes time. You need to remember that as you work toward developing your program. For some clients, I have seen the process take several years—which is why it is so important to follow the recommendations as outlined in the previous chapters.

It's essential to consider the bigger picture and play the long game. Immediate results may not be apparent, but the profound impact on the community will become evident once the program is up and running as intended. As local suppliers gain more opportunities, they contribute to the growth and economic vitality of the community.

By fostering relationships and providing opportunities for local businesses, your supplier diversity program empowers these suppliers to succeed and contribute to the overall economic well-being of their families and communities.

While this all may sound like hyperbole, the results speak for themselves. But again, these things take time. You may not see those results this year, or the next, or even the year after that. But the results will come, and not only will you and your program have made an impact on the community, but your company will have saved money in the process.

In the process of driving supplier diversity goals, it's crucial to consider emotions and provide support for stakeholders throughout the supply chain. Balancing the focus on the end game with addressing potential challenges along the way is essential. It's important to prioritize people because, without their involvement, this job becomes impossible. Avoiding personal attacks and emotional arguments, discussions should revolve around KPIs, economic impact, community engagement, and growth.

By emphasizing data and numbers, the focus shifts away from individual disputes, fostering a more productive and collaborative environment. Staying committed to the long-term vision, while addressing potential roadblocks proactively, will ultimately lead to success in supplier diversity and leave a lasting positive impact on the community and your organization.

It's Not Just the "Right Thing"

It is essential to understand that supplier diversity is not merely a feel-good initiative; instead, it is a strategic business decision with significant economic implications. Numerous studies support this claim—according to a report by the SBA, small businesses accounted for a substantial 44 percent of total US economic activity in 2019. Moreover, these enterprises were responsible for creating an overwhelming 1.5 million net new jobs during the same year, contributing significantly to the nation's employment sector.[15] The Federal Reserve Bank has also revealed that small businesses play an outsized role in fostering economic resilience and innovation.[16] These enterprises are known to drive technological advancements, fueling productivity gains and competitiveness across various industries.

A report from the MBDA also indicated that minority-owned small businesses are a driving force in promoting economic growth in underserved areas.[17] By providing jobs, stimulating local economies, and empowering disadvantaged communities, these enterprises act as agents of positive change.

Furthermore, research from the National Women's Business Council highlights the substantial contribution of women-owned small businesses to the economy. In 2019, there were approximately 12.3

---

15 "Frequently asked questions about small business," 2020, https://advocacy.sba.gov/wp-content/uploads/2020/11/Small-Business-FAQ-2020.pdf.

16 "Small Business and Entrepreneurship," Federal Reserve Board - Small Business and Entrepreneurship, October 19, 2022, https://www.federalreserve.gov/consumer-scommunities/small-business-and-entrepreneurship.htm.

17 "Executive summary - Disparities in capital access between minority and non-minority businesses," Minority Business Development Agency, April 19, 2017, https://archive.mbda.gov/page/executive-summary-disparities-capital-access-between-minority-and-non-minority-businesses.html.

million women-owned businesses in the United States, generating $1.8 trillion in revenue and employing nearly nine million people.[18]

It is evident from these studies that supplier diversity is not about charity or tokenism; it is a strategic imperative for corporations seeking to bolster the economy and foster sustainable growth. By promoting and supporting small and diverse businesses, corporations are investing in the very foundation of the US economy, driving job creation, innovation, and community development.

Supplier diversity is not a side project; it is an integral part of strengthening the nation's economic fabric. Embracing supplier diversity is a win-win scenario for corporations, small businesses, and the economy as a whole. So, let us not undermine its significance by reducing it to a simple act of "doing the right thing." Instead, let us recognize and embrace the transformative power of supplier diversity in driving economic prosperity for all. Today's consumer is a lot more discerning about how they are making buying decisions, and they want to collaborate with corporations that are invested in ESG impact.

Now that acronym has seen some controversy before, but ESG is not about "woke culture" or anything like that. Taken as a whole, ESG is about helping out the community at large. That does not just mean your local area, but as far out as the world itself. The organization's goal is to help, not hinder—and it is a lofty goal for sure.

But it is also there for a reason. Your customers, employees, and even people in management want this. The vast majority of people want to buy from a company that does believe in helping the envi-

---

18   "2020 Annual Report NWBC," National Women's Business Council, December 18, 2020, https://www.nwbc.gov/wp-content/uploads/2020/12/2020-NWBC-Annual-Report.html.

ronment.[19] Employees want to work for a business that does more than just talk about helping those in need, and management sees those demands coming from all over. ESG is not a dirty word, and if your customers want this kind of diversity in your organization, you should give it to them.

Consumers Care About This

Let's face it: Over the past several years, we have seen significant changes in the job market. Between COVID-19, the #MeToo movement, and the death of George Floyd, many employers have reevaluated their relationships with employees. They have also been forced to examine their policies around DEI. A recently published report by Harvard Business Review cited that 67 percent of employers surveyed considered DEI as a high strategic priority.[20]

I often remind my clients that it was not so long ago that the office was a place where women and minorities were harassed on a regular basis. If not for the fact that employers have been intentional about change, we would not be where we are now. DEI is becoming a household term. People expect diversity to be a part of the conversation and culture when they look for work—and when they look for products to purchase.

The modern consumer is no longer solely focused on price and product; they are increasingly discerning and conscious about the

---

19   Solitaire Townsend, "88% of consumers want you to help them make a difference," Forbes, November 21, 2018, https://www.forbes.com/sites/solitairetownsend/2018/11/21/consumers-want-you-to-help-them-make-a-difference/.

20   "Creating a culture of diversity, equity, and inclusion," Society for Human Resource Management, https://shrm.org/hr-today/trends-and-forecasting/research-and-surveys/Documents/DEI%20Metrics%20Full%20Report.pdf.

broader impact of their purchasing decisions. Here's why supporting small businesses through supplier diversity and championing ESG practices makes perfect sense:

1. *Consumer Preferences:* Studies consistently show that consumers prefer to support socially responsible businesses. According to a survey by Cone Communications, 86 percent of consumers are more likely to buy from companies that advocate for social and environmental issues.[21] By integrating supplier diversity and ESG principles, you signal your commitment to sustainable practices, fostering goodwill and loyalty among conscious consumers.

2. *Market Share Growth:* Emphasizing supplier diversity and ESG can open up new market segments. Millennials and Generation Z, as the rising consumer forces, are particularly inclined to support businesses that prioritize environmental and social initiatives. By showcasing your commitment to these values, you can attract and retain this influential demographic, gaining a competitive edge in the market.

3. *Brand Reputation:* Corporate responsibility and ESG have a direct impact on brand reputation. Companies with strong social and environmental records enjoy a more positive public image, leading to increased brand trust and credibility. Your dedication to supplier diversity and ESG can set you apart as an ethical and purpose-driven organization.

4. *Investor Attraction:* Investors are increasingly evaluating companies based on their ESG performance. In fact, ESG

---

21   Libby Maccarthy, "New report reveals 86% of US consumers expect companies to act on social, environmental issues," Sustainable Brands, May 18, 2017, https://sustainablebrands.com/read/marketing-and-comms/new-report-reveals-86-of-us-consumers-expect-companies-to-act-on-social-environmental-issues.

investing has grown exponentially in recent years, with assets managed under ESG criteria reaching trillions of dollars.[22] By showcasing your commitment to supplier diversity and ESG, you can attract socially responsible investors who align with your values and support your growth.

In order to be competitive in today's job market, an employer must offer more than a competitive salary and benefits. Employees care about workplace culture, pay equity, and, in many cases, they want to know their job somehow contributes to the greater good.

Which leads us right back to supplier diversity. If your employees want a workplace that supports the community and various minority populations, these programs are a great fit. Do you really have a sustainable DEI program without thinking about supplier diversity? I certainly do not think so.

This discussion about supplier diversity cannot exist in a silo. It needs to be a part of a larger conversation about corporate responsibility.

It's *Not* Charity Work

One reason why I cringe every time I hear "It is the right thing to do" is because it implies all diverse businesses need help, so the big corporations will just "help" them. That is not the spirit in which I am talking or thinking about supplier diversity.

The existence of numerous programs designed to "help" MWBE can inadvertently perpetuate the idea that these businesses are in constant need of assistance. While these programs do provide valuable

---

22   "Capital Group ESG Global Study 2023," Capital Group, August 31, 2023, https://www.capitalgroup.com/institutional/investments/esg/perspectives/esg-global-study.html.

support, they should not define the core essence of supplier diversity. Instead, supplier diversity is about recognizing the immense potential and value that diverse suppliers bring to the table; it is about fostering economic growth, driving innovation, and cultivating a diverse and inclusive business ecosystem.

The impact of diverse suppliers goes beyond economic benefits. Supplier diversity fosters a culture of inclusion and demonstrates a corporation's commitment to diversity, equity, and social responsibility. It provides opportunities for diverse suppliers to showcase their skills, products, and services on a level playing field, breaking down barriers to entry in the market.

Supplier diversity is not an optional "feel-good" initiative; it is a strategic imperative that positively impacts customer perception and loyalty. When customers see a corporation actively engaging with diverse suppliers, they recognize it as an indication of the company's dedication to serving diverse communities and embracing diverse perspectives.

Beyond economic benefits, supplier diversity drives competition and ensures competitive pricing, which ultimately benefits both the corporation and its customers. By highlighting the value that supplier diversity brings to the table, corporations can build a strong case for its continued support, even in challenging economic times. Let's take a closer look at a real-world example to understand how diverse suppliers can save corporations money while promoting supplier diversity.

A higher education client embarked on a five-year journey to increase their supplier diversity spending. Instead of merely viewing supplier diversity as a philanthropic gesture, they approached it as a strategic initiative to boost engagement with local diverse suppliers and foster healthy competition.

To kickstart their program, the organization conducted a comprehensive analysis of their existing purchases with diverse suppliers. They even sought the assistance of a third party to uncover previously unidentified diverse suppliers, a savvy move that paid off. Surprisingly, they discovered that they were already spending more with diverse suppliers than initially thought. By reframing supplier diversity as an integral part of their procurement process, the university saw a significant upswing in supplier diversity spend.

One of the key tactics they employed was the establishment of a procurement process designed to offer competitive access and sourcing opportunities to a broader pool of qualified bidders. Expanding the pool of potential bidders was crucial, encompassing not only minorities and women but also small LGBTQ+, veteran, and service-disabled veteran businesses. This approach dismantled the misconception that diverse suppliers were less qualified than their non-diverse counterparts, making it clear that supplier diversity is not merely "the right thing to do" but a strategic advantage.

In addition to spending with diverse suppliers, the client adopted a multifaceted approach to measuring success. While spending with diverse suppliers was indeed a metric, it was not the sole focus. They also assessed the relationships and collaborations with diverse suppliers and evaluated how effectively they worked together. This holistic evaluation allowed them to determine the overall success of their supplier diversity program.

So again, the impact of engaging with diverse suppliers goes beyond the idea of "doing the right thing." It offers corporations tangible benefits that contribute to cost savings and operational efficiencies, such as:

1. *Competitive Pricing:* By expanding the pool of potential bidders to include diverse suppliers, corporations introduce

healthy competition into the procurement process. This competition can lead to competitive pricing and better value for goods and services.

2. *Innovation and Creativity:* Diverse suppliers bring fresh perspectives and innovative solutions to the table that can lead to creative problem-solving and the development of unique products or services, ultimately benefiting the corporation and its customers.

3. *Increased Efficiency:* Partnering with diverse suppliers can enhance operational efficiency. These suppliers often have a deep understanding of local markets and can provide faster response times, shorter lead times, and more agile supply chain solutions.

4. *Access to Niche Markets:* Diverse suppliers may have access to niche markets or specialized expertise that can open new business opportunities for corporations. By tapping into these markets, corporations can expand their customer base and revenue streams.

5. *Enhanced Reputation and Customer Loyalty:* Again, today's consumers are increasingly conscious of CSR and ESG initiatives. Engaging with diverse suppliers demonstrates a commitment to diversity and inclusion, which can boost a corporation's reputation and foster customer loyalty.

So no, this isn't charity, and it's not something a company should do because they're told it's the right thing to do. No, this is a solid financial decision for all parties involved, and companies should do it because it helps everyone's bottom lines. By viewing supplier diversity as a means to promote healthy competition, innovation, and access to niche markets, corporations can build a supplier base that drives economic growth and contributes to the overall success of the organization.

Action Plan

Set up meetings and interviews with various stakeholders in your organization to determine their appetite for supplier diversity programs. Then take note of how teammates feel about such programming. Get their ideas and suggestions.

Develop an internal communication plan that speaks to why your organization is implementing a supplier diversity program. Go beyond "It's the right thing to do."

Engage with local partners and community-based organizations to get their insights, feedback, and potential support.

For more information on strategies for communicating with internal and external stakeholders go to
https://jkasolutions.com/diversify&prosper.com

8

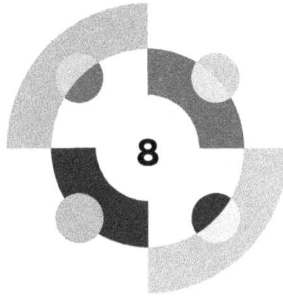

Supplier Diversity and Your Local Community

At this point in the book, you already have a good idea of how a supplier diversity program works, how you should build it, the problems you will face, and how to keep everything running smoothly. But now I want to take a moment to discuss something with a little more focus: your local community.

While I have touched on the specific impacts that a supplier diversity plan can have on your area, I think it is important for you to do the same. The best way I can think of to do that is to continue discussing issues that impact your community, but also to give you multiple examples of how this works in the real world—scenarios where you can see for yourself how the choices you make today will make a dent in your immediate area.

This is what everything is all about. It is the reason why you are doing what you are doing at the end of the day, and it is your motivation to do things the right way the first time. That makes it sound like a bigger deal than it is, and if you are not someone who fits into a category like those I described in chapter one, I get that. If you have never been a minority, then you would not understand what it is like to be one.

The opportunities presented to minority groups as a result of supplier diversity programs like this one are huge. They can help lift families out of poverty. They can empower people to feel like what they do matters, and give them a reason to get up in the morning. Your supplier diversity program has a lot of potential power. It is just up to you to harness it.

With that in mind, start thinking about what your supplier diversity program could do for your community. Let us begin by homing in on strategies.

Strategy for Creating a Sustainable Program

There is not a one-size-fits-all solution to creating a sustainable supplier diversity program. Each situation and company is different, and each community has its own unique nuances and requirements. Things can also change depending on the political climate, economic conditions, and a variety of other factors. When thinking about building your own program, you should consider the long-term implications of the plan and how to address some of the issues that might come up.

I constantly have conversations with companies that are really conflicted. On the one hand, they want to implement these supplier diversity programs, but they're really struggling with figuring out how it is going to impact the big picture: ROI for shareholders. Unfortunately, the majority of people tend to see supplier diversity as charity, and in some cases, a threat to corporate profits.

This is a mindset that needs to change. The best opportunity for you to do so is right at the onset of your program, during the pitch to the C-suite. Call it out on the table: "Supplier diversity is not charity." Then lay out all of the reasons why that statement is true. You then take a lot of the gas out of the charity concept, and hopefully it will not come up later on.

If you need more talking points other than what you have read so far, this chapter will give you some of them through examples. You can use those same case studies to present to the C-suite as evidence to make your case.

As a leader it is important to take these concerns under advisement, otherwise the program is going to fail. If stakeholders see supplier diversity as charity, then it is going to be the first thing that gets cut during an economic downturn. What I tend to advise our clients is to instead shift the mindset to about what would happen if they failed to implement a sustainable program.

I've already talked about how employees feel about these issues, as well as the importance of DEI in your process. One of the hypothetical outcomes of not implementing a sustainable program could be a decreased interest from potential employees. It could be reduced sales as customers move toward companies that do give back. Or it could be as simple as losing out to the competition who is pushing forward these initiatives.

As organizations seek to increase market share, we are seeing an increased demand for ESG to produce long-term value for potential stakeholders. Yet again, this is just one of the potential downsides to not implementing a supplier diversity program, and one that should be focused on.

Stopping the negative thoughts in their tracks is just one way to ensure that the supplier diversity program that you are creating stays sustainable. But now let's take this into the real world with a few examples of companies I have worked with over the years where their supplier diversity program has evolved over time. I can't say this enough: It doesn't happen overnight. There's almost a trial-and-error process that occurs, and you need to be aware of that so you can plan accordingly.

Perspectives from Diverse Suppliers

CASE STUDY

David

In this heartfelt case study, we explore the inspiring journey of David, a determined entrepreneur and refugee who found a new home in the United States. David's story is a shining example of how supplier diversity can transform lives and create a positive impact on local communities. As a concessionaire providing retail, food, and beverage services at airports, David's journey exemplifies the true essence of supplier diversity and its potential to uplift individuals and underserved communities.

Background

When David fled his homeland in search of a better life for his family and arrived in the United States, he faced numerous challenges as an immigrant. However, his perseverance and determination led him to the world of concessionaires—an industry that resonated with his passion for hospitality and customer service.

Opportunity through Supplier Diversity

David's life took a transformative turn when he got the opportunity to operate a restaurant at the airport. This opportunity was intentionally set aside for local businesses through the airport's supplier diversity initiative. The program's commitment to supporting local entrepreneurs like David provided him with the platform he needed to thrive in the competitive concessionaire industry.

Giving Back to the Community

David's story is not just about business success; it is a testament to the power of giving back. During the challenging times of the pandemic, David and his family pivoted their business to provide food to underserved communities. Their dedication to serving others in need exemplifies the profound impact that diverse suppliers can have on the communities they serve.

Empowering Young Lives

One of the most touching moments in David's journey is the story of a nineteen-year-old boy who was homeless and living in a shelter. David offered him a job at the airport restaurant, giving him a chance to rebuild his life. The young man thrived in his new role until transportation challenges posed a threat to his employment. In a display of compassion and support, David offered to lend the young man money to secure an apartment, allowing him to continue working. This act of kindness reflects the core values of supplier diversity—providing opportunities, fostering growth, and uplifting lives.

Supplier Diversity at Its Best

David's story exemplifies the true essence of supplier diversity. It goes beyond merely providing opportunities to diverse suppliers; it's about creating a supportive ecosystem that empowers individuals and strengthens communities. Supplier diversity initiatives like the one that helped David flourish at the airport not only drive economic growth but also cultivate a sense of purpose and responsibility among businesses.

Conclusion

David's journey as a concessionaire showcases the transformative power of supplier diversity in the most profound way. It highlights the importance of intentional efforts to support local businesses, uplift underserved communities, and provide opportunities for those seeking a better life. Through supplier diversity, corporations can make a meaningful impact on people's lives and create a more inclusive and compassionate world for everyone. David's story is a testament to the incredible possibilities that unfold when we embrace the true spirit of supplier diversity.

CASE STUDY

Andrea

Meet Andrea, a tenacious individual who refused to let multiple sclerosis (MS) hinder her determination to succeed. Her inspiring journey showcases the transformative power of supplier diversity and its impact on communities. Despite facing personal challenges, Andrea's story demonstrates the significance of creating opportunities for diverse suppliers and the profound effect it can have on people's lives.

Background

Andrea was once thriving in a corporate job, until an unexpected diagnosis of MS changed the course of her life. She experienced fluctuating energy levels, mobility issues, and speech difficulties. Doctors advised her to consider disability and step away from work, but Andrea had a different vision for her future. Undeterred by adversity, she decided to forge her path as an entrepreneur.

The Entrepreneurial Leap

Launching her marketing agency, Andrea embarked on a journey that would not only transform her life but also her community. Although she started small, she recognized the potential benefits of supplier diversity programs. Getting certified as an MWBE opened doors to government agencies and large corporations, providing her with significant growth opportunities.

Community Impact

As Andrea's agency flourished, she realized that her success had a broader impact. By becoming an employer in her local town, she could make a difference in people's lives. Offering competitive salaries and full benefits, Andrea created job opportunities for her community, empowering individuals to build better futures for themselves and their families.

The Power of Making Opportunities Available

Andrea's journey exemplifies the importance of making opportunities available to diverse suppliers. Supplier diversity programs not only drive business growth but also empower individuals from diverse backgrounds to thrive in the competitive market. Through these programs, underrepresented entrepreneurs like Andrea can access networks, resources, and mentorship that fuel their success.

A Voice for Change

In addition to her entrepreneurial journey, Andrea embraced her role as an advocate for MS awareness. Collaborating with large pharmaceutical companies—some of whom were her clients—she actively engaged with the MS community, offering hope and inspiration to others facing similar challenges.

Supplier Diversity and Community Empowerment

Andrea's story highlights the profound connection between supplier diversity and community empowerment. By providing opportunities to diverse suppliers, corporations contribute to building resilient communities and fostering economic growth. Supplier diversity is not merely a business strategy but a driving force for positive social impact.

Conclusion

Andrea's remarkable journey showcases the transformative power of supplier diversity programs and their ability to create meaningful change. Through her resilience, determination, and the support of supplier diversity initiatives, she not only built a successful business but also made a lasting impact on her community. The case of Andrea is a testament to the importance of making opportunities available to diverse suppliers and the profound ripple effect it can have on society. Embracing supplier diversity is not just about doing business; it's about empowering communities and transforming lives.

CASE STUDY

Johnny

Johnny's journey is a testament to the resilience of the human spirit and the transformative power of a mentor–protégé relationship. From facing homelessness to building a thriving janitorial business, Johnny's story highlights the crucial role of support, guidance, and supplier diversity programs in empowering individuals to succeed even amidst the most challenging circumstances.

Background

Johnny once had a flourishing business until his life took an unexpected turn when he became a caregiver for an aging relative. Balancing the demands of caregiving with running a business proved to be overwhelming, and Johnny's business eventually suffered, leading to his departure from the company he once built. His life took a difficult turn, and he found himself homeless, struggling to regain his footing in society.

Emerging from Adversity

Despite facing immense challenges, Johnny refused to be defeated. He took on odd jobs to sustain himself and eventually found the inspiration to start anew. Johnny launched a janitorial firm, driven by his work ethic and determination to rebuild his life.

The Struggle to Thrive

Starting his janitorial business, Johnny faced the uphill battle of finding clients and establishing a steady stream of income. He poured his heart and soul into his venture, working tirelessly to make ends meet.

The Turning Point

Johnny's fortune changed when he learned about supplier diversity programs and the potential they held for his business. Recognizing the value of certification, he pursued the necessary qualifications, which opened doors to corporate clients seeking diverse suppliers.

Entering a Mentor–Protégé Relationship

As Johnny's janitorial firm grew, he sought opportunities to learn and refine his business practices. He entered into a mentor–protégé relationship with an experienced business leader who offered invaluable guidance and support. Through this partnership, Johnny gained insights into scaling his business, improving operations, and fostering customer relationships.

Thriving with Corporate Clients

Armed with newfound knowledge and experience, Johnny's janitorial firm flourished. Corporate clients recognized the quality of his services and the dedication he brought to his work. The mentor–protégé relationship played a pivotal role in Johnny's ability to not only secure but also retain these valuable corporate contracts.

The Power of Supplier Diversity

For Johnny, supplier diversity was more than a business opportunity; it was a lifeline that helped him rebuild his life and thrive despite adversity. Supplier diversity programs provided him with access to networks, support, and mentorship, enabling him to grow his business and establish a stable foundation for his future.

Conclusion

Johnny's remarkable journey from homelessness to entrepreneurial success exemplifies the transformative impact of a mentor–protégé relationship and the power of supplier diversity programs. Despite facing daunting challenges, Johnny's resilience, combined with the support of mentorship and supplier diversity initiatives, allowed him to rise above adversity and build a thriving janitorial business. His story is a testament to the potential of supplier diversity to create life-changing opportunities for individuals, fostering growth, empowerment, and lasting impact in their lives.

Market Research

Much of the process begins with market research. You might not realize how important this process is. After all, you are making your supply chain more diverse. Why would you need to go out and determine what the marketplace is like? Why is that important?

I've brought this up in previous chapters, but it's an important reminder: Before you start to implement your supplier diversity plan, you have got to really understand what is happening in the marketplace.

For example, look at what happened in 2022 and 2023. Unemployment was an issue, as was inflation. Gas prices started out high, dipped low, then got high again. All of these things matter and will affect how you implement your system. Think about it from the supplier's perspective. If you are trucking in all of your wares, then the cost of gasoline and diesel fuel going up is going to directly impact the cost of their goods. If they do not have enough employees to work for them, they may not deliver items on time.

Market research is looking at where you are in terms of economics—inflation, gas costs, etc.—and what kind of supplier diversity program you want to create. Is it about increasing opportunities? How does that impact shareholders if you are in a publicly traded company? What is the availability of local and diverse suppliers? That is all really important.

We've already discussed how oftentimes there is a disconnect between procurement teams and folks who want to implement these supplier diversity programs, and market research helps push some of these issues into the light. This is something that you want to rectify right off the bat. A considerable amount of time should be given to getting the teams in alignment. Otherwise, they will butt heads, slowing down or even stopping the system before it starts.

With some of our clients, we have seen strategies that they call a contingency. The procurement team knows that there might be instances where there is a focus on local, and that is OK. After all, they know about this contingency beforehand.

Price cannot be your only deciding factor. Local and diverse suppliers cannot compete with national companies. It is not a matter of skills, either. It is a matter of volume. Larger companies get discounts, have access to different things, and can operate at a different scale. It becomes really difficult to implement a supplier diversity program if price is the only metric that matters, and sometimes that is the only metric that matters to the procurement team.

Just having those conversations between teams is really important. It helps align expectations, and if you have done the market research beforehand, then everyone is really on the same page. This transparency should trickle down to the diverse suppliers as well. Having them really understand the needs of your organization and engagement with the community is essential.

Economic Impact

When you are creating a sustainable supplier diversity program, you want to be thinking about the metrics—both good and bad—and their economic impact. You need to make very clear that there could be upsides and downsides that could affect your stockholders, your C-suite, your employees, and so on.

For example, today's employees are very concerned with impact. As we discussed, they want to work for organizations that align with their personal values. Therefore, creating a supplier diversity program can become part of your talent strategy. It could help you attract and retain the best talent.

I believe the same is true for customers. I have conversations with business associate friends of mine, and they will not work with companies that do not have a commitment to diversity. Case in point: I went into an athletic wear store recently, where I was looking for some new running shoes. I was just browsing around, and then I decided to go home. I like to order stuff online anyway, and this particular store had a website I could peruse at my leisure. But when I did, I did not see any diversity on their website at all. It wasn't just race and gender. There was just one particular body type and race represented by this particular brand, and I chose not to buy from them because I was almost insulted to see there was no commitment to any type of diversity. There's your economic impact right there.

Your supplier diversity program needs to take account for these kinds of things. Yes, that can seem like a daunting task when you are starting out, and I get that. However, do your best to account for as many variables as you can, with economic impact being one of them. You will be glad that you did.

Accountability and Compliance

Now let's talk about some recommendations to promote account-ability. Transparency and open communication are really important. A lot of these supplier diversity programs happen behind closed doors because companies are afraid of saying or doing the wrong thing. And if they are not successful, they worry the backlash will be severe. If you and your company are going to do something, whether it's standing up for the Black community after a prominent death, such as what happened to George Floyd, you have to be purposeful and clear about it. And if you do struggle or have difficulty, if it is not perfect, be open about the problems and engage in some of the strategies that I've shared.

Whatever you do, do not say you are going to implement this supplier diversity program and then not be clear about what it is, how outside vendors engage with you, and what you are selling. Transparency in every aspect of the program is key.

I also recommend compliance reviews. This is something that an organization like mine, or another third party, could accomplish. All of the big management consulting firms have some kind of compliance program where they can come in and help you make your own program, and you can take advantage of that as well.

Credible compliance reviews are very important because even companies with the best intentions make mistakes. For example, I once had a client who highlighted a large company and said, "This is a woman-owned business." My partner and I looked the company up, checked out the website, and wondered, is it? Turns out the company was promoting themselves as a woman-owned business, but they weren't actually certified, and after conducting due diligence we learned that the company was not owned and operated by women. Compliance reviews would help solve this problem.

You also have to address fraud. As unfortunate as it is, I have seen businesses that represent themselves as women-owned to get the benefits, when they were actually fronts for male-owned companies. We have seen clients go through this very process of finding a company, seeing they were an MWBE, only to find out that it was not legit.

Checks and balances in your program are important, as are the accompanying metrics. Find out what kinds of firms are winning and why, because then you can follow their lead.

Throughout this chapter, we have delved into the powerful connection between supplier diversity and its profound impact on local communities. The case studies of Vinny's thriving concessionaire business and Johnny's janitorial firm demonstrate the tremendous potential that arises when local and diverse suppliers are given opportunities to shine.

These case studies illustrate that when local and diverse suppliers are given opportunities, they are not only able to succeed but also compelled to reach back and support their communities. Their success echoes beyond their businesses, nurturing a thriving ecosystem of economic growth and empowerment. The economic impact of supporting small local suppliers cannot be underestimated, as they create jobs, stimulate local economies, and foster a sense of community pride.

As businesses embrace supplier diversity programs and provide opportunities for local and diverse suppliers, they become catalysts for positive social change. Through collaborative efforts, we can build a future where communities are uplifted, economies thrive, and diverse voices are heard, making the world a better place for everyone. The journey to harnessing the full potential of supplier diversity continues, and it holds the promise of a brighter and more inclusive future for all.

Action Plan

1. Create your strategy for developing your supplier diversity program. Will you stagger your goals or go all in?
2. Develop your communication plan for how you will relay everything about your program so everyone is properly informed.
3. Perform market research in your area. Look for places to be your vendors.

For more information about conducting market research, go to https://jkasolutions.com/diversify&prosper.com

Conclusion

One of the main reasons why I wrote this book is because I have seen a lot of companies try and fail at creating a sustainable supplier diversity program. As I am sure you understand at this point, when talking about a sustainable program, I am referring to one that has measurable impact. Year after year I have seen companies talk about their supplier diversity goals, percentages, and spending, but it is rare that we hear about the people who have been impacted, or the true economic impact of the program.

When I think about supplier diversity, it is personal. As a minority and woman business owner myself, I had to learn to change and adapt my thinking about supplier diversity to be more inclusive. After all, how can we talk about a sustainable supplier diversity program when we only include minorities and women? A true supplier diversity program needs to consider its impact on the local community, and this may vary depending on industry and location. I remind my clients that an inclusive program takes into account local small businesses, minorities, women, service-disabled veterans, people with disabilities, the formerly incarcerated, and really any underserved or marginalized group.

You might be thinking that with all the different groups, politics, and variables, what exactly is the best way to create a sustainable supplier diversity plan? That's why I have talked in this book about avoiding the desire to create a one-size-fits-all plan. Creating a system requires careful planning. It starts with determining the reason for the plan in the first place and figuring out the goal. Asking yourself, "Why create a supplier diversity plan now?" The bottom line is—and this may be awkward to talk about—cancel culture is a thing. Supplier diversity is becoming increasingly important to consumers, and not addressing it in a thoughtful way could have a negative impact on your business.

If you don't pay attention to your local community and don't prioritize diversity as a matter of policy, you could end up on the wrong side of an argument—and potentially lose business. Stopping that from happening is pretty straightforward, too: Pay attention to your community and support local organizations.

The consequences of not embracing supplier diversity can be severe and far-reaching. In today's world, where consumers are becoming more socially conscious and expect businesses to reflect their values, a misalignment with diversity and inclusion messaging can lead to significant backlash and damage to a company's reputation.

Take the example of Nike, a global brand that faced backlash from consumers who chose to boycott the company due to controversies surrounding figures like Colin Kaepernick. The brand's missteps in understanding and respecting different cultures, such as the mishandling of Asian culture representation, also contributed to negative sentiments and lost customers.

Not only can a lack of commitment to supplier diversity lead to consumer backlash, but it can also result in legal troubles. Companies like Abercrombie & Fitch, Walmart, and General Electric have faced lawsuits for racial discrimination, highlighting the importance of creating an inclusive and diverse business environment that extends beyond just external suppliers.

Moreover, not embracing supplier diversity can hinder a company's ability to tap into new markets and engage with diverse consumer bases. By overlooking diverse suppliers, a company may miss out on unique insights, innovative solutions, and competitive pricing, ultimately weakening its market position and losing potential customers.

CASE STUDY

New Haven, Connecticut

As of July 2022, the town of New Haven, Connecticut, had 138,915 residents. Of those, 40 percent were white; 33.9 percent were Black; 5.2 percent were Asian; 30.3 percent were Hispanic or Latino; and 7.5 percent were another racial group or combination of two or more. In total, when you add up all of the various demographic groups, 76.6 percent of the population is not white.[23]

The city's chamber of commerce, however, did not reflect that reality.

When Jesse Steven Phillips became a member, he knew that there was work to be done. He previously worked at the National Urban League, the NAACP, and in local politics. The chamber of commerce, however, presented a different challenge. "You probably could count on your hand how many Black people were

---

23 US Census Bureau, "QuickFacts: New Haven City, Connecticut," accessed September 2023, https://www.census.gov/quickfacts/fact/table/newhavencityconnecticut/PST045222.

members of the chamber. And even with Latinos as well, I mean, it just didn't exist," Phillips told me in an interview.

"Folks do see themselves in the New Haven proper community, because it is a minority-majority city," Phillips says. "I mean, it is culturally rich, like all different, so it is like you see yourself out there. It was like, 'All right, why don't we see ourselves in [the Chamber of Commerce]?'"

For the uninitiated, this might not make sense. You can be part of a community and never interact with the local chamber of commerce. What makes this situation different?

"The only way you create wealth is through business ownership and entrepreneurship," Phillips says. Which means if the local population doesn't see themselves represented in the chamber, then they may not feel comfortable starting a business. After all, that is what the chamber of commerce does: support small businesses and help them succeed. This, therefore, means people who want to succeed and start their own business may never actually do so. If people with different diverse backgrounds didn't see representations of themselves in the chamber, then it felt to them like they weren't a part of the business community. This suppressed people from actually starting their own companies, just out of fear. As an example, Black children who grow up today know they have the ability to be president someday, because of the legacy of President Barack Obama. But women may not feel the same way, because there has never been a woman in that office.

And to the credit of the Greater New Haven Chamber of Commerce, this was a subject they were starting to tackle head-on, but it wasn't happening fast enough.

Phillips took on the role of Coordinator of Inclusive Growth, and his job is to coordinate and implement their inclusive growth strategy within the chamber. It is a complex position that involves systemic issues of economic inclusion and participation, plus access to capital. I met him when we worked together on the New Haven Diversity and Inclusion Committee.

Thanks to the efforts of many of the members of the chamber of commerce, including Phillips, the membership has grown more diverse. Current leadership has accepted the mistakes the chamber has made in the past and is moving forward. By bringing these issues to light, they make topics like racism and a lack of diversity more important.

"So, in your silence, you also support it, you know?" Phillips says. "And that's the problem. I think that's more of the struggle we have to deal with than making people feel uncomfortable. You know, we can't have you guys silent, because silent means you accept that you don't see anything wrong."

By continuing to show the community that the New Haven Chamber of Commerce does reflect the values and makeup of the community, they're making a difference on the population at large.

"We want you to be at the table," Phillips says.

As you explore creating a supplier diversity program, my recommendation is to base the plan on reasonable goals and expectations. Start with the data, look at what you are spending and how you are spending. Think about where the greatest opportunities for success are. As you explore that thought, remember that opportunities need to match up with the availability of qualified, local suppliers. That's another area that requires focus: What is a qualified supplier? I have talked about the importance of creating a standard for vendors that reduces risk to your organization while taking into consideration how small businesses generally work. To be clear, I am not talking about lowering standards. I am discussing what is reasonable and necessary when working with small businesses.

I also think it's important to understand the nuances between small businesses and corporations. Small businesses operate totally different in terms of day-to-day operations, financials, and even managerial styles. Some of my most successful small business clients run multiple seven- and eight-figure businesses that are family owned and operated, and while they are very successful, they struggle with cash flow management, banking relationships, and back-office operations. While I won't speak for all small businesses, I do see many successful small firms that are run by husband-and-wife teams that include other family members. I share this to say that to emphasize how the dynamics of running a small business can be different from larger corporations.

Don't make the mistake of trying to create a supplier diversity program that treats small, diverse suppliers like big businesses. Instead, think about some things you can do to ensure your program is successful.

Ultimately, you can do everything right in terms of planning, market research, etc., but the plan will not succeed without a strong commitment from senior leadership. All too often we see companies set goals that fail because there is a disconnect between supplier diversity goals, procurement, and other KPIs. Effective leadership means that a sustainable supplier diversity program is part of a procurement plan and part of the company's KPIs. It also means that the C-suite is visible and they talk about supplier diversity as a policy, whether they are speaking to board members or the community. No matter what, the message is the same.

Well-qualified diverse suppliers are in high demand, and this call for diverse suppliers is only going to increase as more companies start implementing their ESG strategies. To stand out you should start thinking about diverse suppliers in the same way you think about your employee talent pipeline. The strategy becomes more focused on attracting and retaining the best talent/supplier. This type of a strategy is long term; it requires a real effort and constant reinforcement. One of the ways that we approach this is through a guided communication plan for both internal and external stakeholders. Internal stakeholders need to understand exactly what we are doing and why, and there needs to be a strong and clear message to external stakeholders and members of the community that the plan is serious—it's not just checking boxes. You must focus on building trust. The community watches and sees everything.

It can take a while to build trust both inside and outside of the organization, which is why my recommendation is to focus on defining a clear process that everyone can follow. Throughout the book I've shared examples of ways that you can differentiate your program so that it resonates with diverse suppliers. We talked about having smaller contracts set aside that would enable smaller local firms to engage with your organization, and about looking at everyday purchases; things that may not go through a procurement process—

things like ordering lunch or purchasing supplies—and finding ways to be more intentional about engagement with small business. Of course, there is your process and finally, and often most important, your payment process. Vendors need to know that if they work with you, they are going to be paid on time.

It's been my experience that once a corporation starts working with a good diverse supplier, they want to give them more work. This is great but requires thoughtful consideration. Large corporations can often pull from an abundance of resources when they want to expand; it's different for small businesses. Talk with these suppliers and include them in discussions about capacity and expansion. There are so many options that are available when partners work together.

I know what you are thinking: This all sounds great, but if it's that easy then why don't we see and hear about more success stories? Quite frankly, it is because of resistance. One of the biggest issues I see in corporations is the reluctance to change. Remember, to develop and maintain a successful supplier diversity program, you must change. Simple. So remember my words that one of the greatest barriers to a successful supplier diversity program is change management. People get comfortable with their existing vendors and processes—no one likes or wants to change it. Change management is part of the process.

Think about all the reasons that folks don't want to do this. It's going to cost too much money, we don't have time, it's hard. I've even had clients who were reluctant to start a program because they were afraid of public perception about the fact that they were not more diverse. When I come up against this resistance, I recommend focusing on what we know works well in a corporate environment and that's focusing on KPIs and data. You can't argue with facts, so always remember to focus on data, and do the necessary market research to determine the availability of qualified suppliers. When creating your program include information about economic impact, job creation, and risk mitigation—what could happen if you don't do this work, or don't have a real plan for inclusion?

As I wrap up my thoughts, I just want to thank you for taking the time to dive into this topic with me. For over four decades, I've been involved with supplier diversity work in some capacity or another, and what I've learned over the years is that all of this is really about inclusion. It's about taking responsibility for our role in society and thinking about how our actions impact our communities, our neighbors, and even future generations. Think about all the good work that has been done in the DEI space. We are finally starting to see and experience the impact of a more inclusive workplace. My hope is that those lessons translate into a more inclusive supply chain as well.

About the Author

With nearly four decades of experience in the business world, Jean Kristensen has emerged as a beacon of change and progress. Her journey, from an early career as a marketing manager at Thompson Financial Services to her current role as a leader in supplier diversity and economic inclusion, is a testament to her unwavering dedication and passion.

In the 1980s, Jean faced a pivotal decision—to continue her career in the financial sector or embrace a new path. She chose the latter, joining her family's security guard firm. Little did she know that this choice would become the cornerstone of her remarkable professional voyage.

Working closely with her family's business, Jean witnessed firsthand the transformative power of supplier diversity programs. These initiatives didn't just elevate her family's firm into a multimillion dollar success story; they also had a profound impact on the lives of their employees and the community they served. It was during this time that Jean realized the true potential of supplier diversity—it wasn't merely a business strategy; it was a catalyst for wealth creation, forging connections, and opening doors to previously unimagined opportunities.

Jean's list of accolades is as impressive as it is extensive. Driven by her passion for supplier diversity, she became an advocate for other diverse suppliers, guiding them to access opportunities with major corporations and government agencies. Her tireless efforts have earned her numerous recognitions, including a place on City & State magazine's MWBE Power 50 list and the prestigious Equity & Inclusion Opportunity Award from the Greater New Haven Chamber of Commerce. Additionally, she has been honored as one of the Top Women to Watch in Real Estate.

In May 2007, Jean founded JKA Supplier Diversity Solutions, a company deeply rooted in her vision of bridging the wealth gap in underserved communities by facilitating their access to opportunities with major corporations and government agencies. Her work with the private sector encompasses a wide range of services, including supplier diversity consulting, outreach, and compliance. With a proven track record, JKA has partnered with corporations across various sectors, including aviation, construction, healthcare, finance, and higher education, making a significant impact on supplier diversity initiatives.

Jean's expertise extends beyond traditional consulting. She has developed comprehensive curriculum and capacity-building programs tailored to diverse suppliers, ensuring their successful participation in supplier diversity programs.

Beyond her professional endeavors, Jean is an active contributor to her community. She dedicates her time to educating small businesses about government contracts and actively supports organizations and nonprofits dedicated to uplifting underserved communities. Her advocacy also extends to health and wellness, where she participates in charity events to raise awareness for breast cancer and multiple sclerosis.

Jean's philanthropic spirit shines through her support for local charities, particularly through her holiday season initiatives with the United Way, where she brings joy and kindness to families in need.

Jean Kristensen is a loving wife, a proud mother of two, and a doting grandmother to three. As the oldest of five siblings and the cherished aunt of numerous nieces and nephews, Jean embraces her role as an exemplar, determined to inspire generations to come.

Jean Kristensen resides in Connecticut, where she shares her life with her husband, and two loyal canine companions. Her journey epitomizes the possibilities that unfold when passion converges with purpose, and her story serves as an inspiration to all who strive to effect positive change through the transformative power of supplier diversity and economic inclusion.

www.ingramcontent.com/pod-product-compliance
Lightning Source LLC
Chambersburg PA
CBHW021926190326
41519CB00009B/926